CONCILIUM

CONCILIUM 2003/1

RETHINKING MARTYRDOM

Edited by
Teresa Okure, Jon Sobrino and Felix Wilfred

SCM Press · London

Published by SCM Press, 9–17 St Albans Place, London N1 0NX

Copyright © Stichting Concilium

English translations copyright © 2003 SCM-Canterbury Press Ltd

All rights reserved. No part of this publication may be
reproduced, stored in a retrieval system, or transmitted,
in any form or by any means, electronic, mechanical, photocopying,
recording or otherwise, without the prior written permission of
Stichting Concilium, Erasmusplein 1,
6525 HT Nijmegen, The Netherlands

ISBN 0 334 03077 2

Printed by Biddles Ltd, Guildford and King's Lynn

Concilium Published February, April, June, October
December

Contents

Introduction
    TERESA OKURE, JON SOBRINO AND FELIX WILFRED   7

I. The Reality of the Martyrs and Victims in Our World

Our World: Cruelty and Compassion
    JON SOBRINO   15

Martyrdom in an Asian Struggle for Life and Dignity: Tamils in Sri Lanka
    S. J. EMMANUEL   24

Martyrs of Latin America
    ELSA TAMEZ   31

Africa, a Martyred Continent: Seed of a New Humanity
    TERESA OKURE, SHCJ   38

II. A Critical Reinterpretation of Martyrdom in the Light of Scripture and Tradition

Jesus the Martyr
    SEÁN FREYNE   49

Witnesses to Love, Killed by Hatred of Love
    JOSÉ IGNACIO GONZÁLEZ FAUS   59

The Servant of Yahweh: The Patient Endurance of the Poor, Mirror of God's Justice
    CARLOS MESTERS   67

Martyrdom in Religious Traditions
   Félix Wilfred   75

III. The Historical Ambiguity of Martyrdom in the Religions

The Problem of Martyrdom in Missionary Countries
   Georg Evers   87

Christians' Responsibility in Situations of Violence: A Challenge for Churches
   Peter Kanyandago   96

Suffering Because of the Church: A Key Issue for Contemporary Catholicism
   Alberto Melloni   106

IV. The Struggle and Hope that Make Martyrs

The Crucified People as 'Light for the Nations': A Reflection on Ignacio Ellacuría
   Kevin F. Burke   123

The Hope Born of the Martyrs' Love
   Juan Hernández Pico   131

Martyrs: An Appeal to the Church
   Jon Sobrino   139

Open Letter to Our Martyrs
   Pedro Casaldáliga   149

Contributors   152

Introduction

TERESA OKURE, JON SOBRINO AND FELIX WILFRED

In March 1983 *Concilium* published a single-issue volume (no. 163 in the English edition) on 'Martyrdom Today'. The reason for tackling the subject then was the appearance of 'a new historico-cultural type of martyrdom', as Johann-Baptist Metz and Edward Schillebeeckx wrote in their Introduction. Twenty years later we are returning to the same subject, since the present situation once more requires a general re-think, and this by its nature involves 're-thinking martyrdom'. This does not mean that everything in our world has changed, but the actual situation, on the one hand, provides new examples and trends, while, on the other hand, there is a new taking stock of this situation. From this viewpoint, and with regard to re-thinking martyrdom, we should like to make three points in this Introduction.

1. Responsive mercy in a cruel world. The first point that makes us think is that, twenty years after that volume on martyrdom, the world as a whole remains unjust, inhuman, and cruel – in some respects more so than then. Under the free-market banner, with its slogan of self-interest, the world is producing immense violence and dealing death to millions of human beings. And globalization – even with its potential for good – has not changed things much but is still producing poverty, oppression, exclusion, and victimization and doing so on the scale of millions. Besides this, we have to recognize that, above all today, ethnic conflicts – complex, ambiguous, and often violent as they are – often overlay injustices perpetrated on minority groups and defenceless tribes.

The fact is, though, that this situation produces people who respond with mercy to defend the victims of the economic order, and for this reason they are violently and unjustly killed without being able to mount any defence. And there are also those who, in the midst of ethnic conflicts, work and struggle to overcome differences and to defend the human rights of the most oppressed. Not everything in these conflicts is 'terrorism', as some would lead us to believe. Many people go to the length of giving up their own lives for the weakest. All the deaths mentioned are above all an expression of love for the poor and the victims, and their exceptional nature stems from this love. Even if we do not give such people a particular title, they are responsively merciful to the end.

This is the major fact that prompts us to 're-think martyrdom' today. There is no counting those who have offered their own lives out of love for the poor, the oppressed, and the despised in the hope that their sacrifice will produce life, justice, and dignity. This means that martyrdom suffered on account of mercy is, first of all, a universal reality: in Latin America this happens above all among Christians; in Asia and other continents, among those who belong to other religions – sometimes among those who do not belong to any religion.

This first reflection strikes us as important not so much for giving honour to individuals as for imitating them in their commitment to truth, love, human rights, and justice in a world so much in need of all these. And this universality of 'martyrdom', understood in this sense, can also act as a utopian principle and as a verdict around which a human globalization, neither selfish nor excluding, can take shape.

Moving on to consider these martyrs specifically from within the biblical-Christian tradition, we call them 'Jesus martyrs', because they die like Jesus and because they have lived, worked, and struggled as he did. They show no trace of 'sacrificialism', or of fanaticism, or even of any directly mystical intention of identifying themselves with the Crucified One. At the heart of their actions is a love of the poor like that shown by Jesus and a defence of the oppressed like that practised by Jesus. Death is an inevitable by-product, not sought but accepted freely out of this love and defence. They do point to a hope, which is not directly that of a reward beyond death but the hope that justice will be done to the victims. If these people are Christians they are martyrs *in* the church but not, strictly speaking, martyrs *of* the church, which shows that, also from within the biblical-Christian tradition, martyrdom is seen as a universal and ecumenical reality. They are martyrs of humankind.

This reality, newly appreciated today, receives an overall treatment in the first article by Jon Sobrino. The articles by S. J. Emmanuel, Elsa Tamez, and Teresa Okure provide concrete examples from the specific circumstances of Asia, Latin America, and Africa. In more analytical mode, Seán Freyne examines what we have called the 'Jesus dimension' from a biblical standpoint in considering the death of Jesus, and José Ignacio González Faus puts forward love as the interpretative key to martyrdom.

2. Suicide and terrorism. The second point requiring thought is the age-old problem, given fresh impetus today, of the outbreak of terrorism, which has connections with the historical embodiments of religions. It is a well-known fact that religions, which claim to be bearers of something absolute, can come to defend this something absolutely, which can involve violence. They can also induce their members to be prepared, and even willing, to give their lives in defence of this absolute. This carries with it the double danger of generating the fanaticism of suicide (often undertaken from belief in a reward after death) and of using suicide to bring about the death of innocent people. This means that we have to be critical of any sort of exaltation of death based on such premises. This is what the article by Felix Wilfred examines.

Together with this most extreme sort of ambiguity, that of martyrdom, we recognize three other examples of ambiguity that continuously recur in the history of the church. The first is the use – often self-interested or ideologized – of the concept of 'martyr' in so-called mission territories, as Georg Evers examines in his article. The second is the question posed to a church that speaks of its own martyrs: whether, historically, it has been on the side of the victims or the victimizers, as Peter Kanyandago analyses. The third and final question is that asked by Alberto Melloni, concerning the persecution and martyrdom inflicted throughout history within the church itself, as exemplified by the persecution of theologians in the twentieth and the present centuries.

3. Giving a name to the crucified peoples. The last subject to concern us is that the most flagrant aspect of the world, with which we began this Introduction, the cruelty that deals death to millions of human beings, is not taken seriously by society or by the church and is very often ignored by theology in its re-thinking of martyrdom. We are speaking of the deaths of millions of people, especially of children, in what used to be called Third World countries, in the form of poverty, exclusion, wars, massacres, in the everyday form of hunger in sub-Saharan countries (Somalia, Eritrea, and others) and in some regions of Asia, of deaths from AIDS, particularly those of children, who are in no way to blame . . . What is happening is undeniable, but the church and theology do not even give these victims a name, let alone grant any sort of dignity to these deaths.

There is nevertheless an incipient process of taking stock of the problem and of the need to find a solution, since what is at stake for humanity is a minimum of decency, while what is at stake for the Christian faith is its very identity and relevance. More specifically, there are two reasons for dealing with this subject in a volume on 'martyrdom'.

The first is historical in nature. These masses of people share with the 'martyrs' the fact that they suffer death, indefensibly and unjustly, sometimes slowly through hunger and oppression, sometimes violently in wars and massacres imposed on them. The second reason is deeper and can ultimately be grasped only from a particular faith, certainly from biblically-based faith: these millions of people are 'the suffering Servant of Yahweh' in our world. In the language of the New Testament, they are 'the crucified Christ'.

The term used to designate these millions of human beings can be debated, but what cannot be done is to leave them without a name in a distant and everlasting anonymity, since they are, according to biblical-Christian faith, the chosen ones of God. If one asks technically whether the term 'martyr' fits them or not in the strict sense, we can perhaps say this: compared to the martyrdom of Jesus, these deaths are *less* of an expression of defence of the poor, of struggle against the anti-kingdom, of fidelity in the midst of persecution, and of freedom in facing death; they are, however *more* of an expression of historical innocence and defencelessness. As is said in the first article, 'they are a *better* expression of the fact that these masses of people are those who are unjustly burdened with a sin that has gradually destroyed them in life and has finally annihilated them in death'.

Silencing these deaths, in society or in the church, not living and giving one's life to bring these crucified peoples down from the cross, is a sin of *lèse*-humanity. While they remain on the cross, we have to show them sorrow, compassion, and reverence. But in addition to this, even though it goes against the grain of instrumental reason and even beyond all compassionate reason, we have to show them gratitude for what the crucified people offer the world of abundance. This is what the article by Carlos Mesters sets out in biblical terms. And if we take the 'Jesus martyrs' and the 'crucified peoples' together, this martyrial reality provides the world with light (Kevin Burke), hope (Juan Hernández Pico), and an appeal (Jon Sobrino).

Faced with the 'lack of meaning' or 'meaninglessness' taking control of more and more people, especially in wealthy societies, the martyrs teach us a great lesson: living is learning to suffer with grace, with elegance; to struggle, certainly, but at the same accepting suffering and tragedy without hatred or loss of hope. This 'martyrial' attitude should be inherent in and constitutive of all authentic spirituality. Martyrdom should not, then, be seen as an extraordinary sacrifice reserved to a few. It is an ideal for a humane spirituality pervading all human actions.

Introduction

In order to give some idea of this, this volume ends with a poem by Pedro Casaldáliga. Rather than re-think martyrdom conceptually, it communicates what he has seen, thought, and experienced over the course of many years. With no trace of masochism or sacrificialism, with the joy of giving life to all, even to one's enemies, and not taking it from anyone, with commitment, gratitude, and hope, this is what he expresses in his 'Open Letter to Our Martyrs'.

Translated by Paul Burns

I. The Reality of the Martyrs and Victims in Our World

Our World: Cruelty and Compassion

JON SOBRINO

Jeremiah, Socrates, Polycarp, Agatha, Joan of Arc, soldiers – possibly, according to St Thomas –, 'the red martyr' discussed by Bloch, Maria Goretti, Fr Kolbe, Gandhi, the theologians Bonhoeffer and Ellacuría, Martin Luther King, Mirna Mack who upheld human rights in Guatemala, Bishop Bukavu of Munzihirwa . . . all these have in common the fact of acceptance of suffering a violent death for the sake of a faith or a cause. Different religions and humanist ideologies bestow special 'dignity' and 'excellence' on their deaths, regardless of the terms used to describe them. For them to be called 'martyrs', it is generally required that the victims should not have acted violently.

I have begun with this list in order to show that martyrdom – whatever definition is given to it – is a historical concept. To 'rethink' it, we need to examine the context that produces it and the reasons it does so. I also want to extend this examination to include the great masses of people who are killed unjustly, whether violently or slowly, who are not generally taken into account when talking of 'martyrdom'.

The background to my considerations is what has happened in Latin America over the past decades in the Third World, notably in Latin America, where 'martyrdom' has been brought about not for religious reasons but for historical, social, military, political and economic ones. I am writing basically out of the biblical-Jesus tradition, the Latin American experience, and knowledge of similar situations in **Africa and Asia**.

I. The world today: victims, victimizers, and compassion

A world of victims and victimzers. Auschwitz, Hiroshima, and the Gulags are behind us, but millions of human beings continue to suffer massively, unjustly, and innocently in repressions, wars, and massacres. Many millions more suffer a slow death from poverty, particularly women and children, besides the death of their dignity and their cultures. . . So-called globalization has not changed things; it has rather increased the numbers of 'excluded'. Two figures from the present: 1,300 million people live on less than a dollar a day; in the Democratic Republic of Congo around three million have died over the past four years in a war provoked by powerful nations for control of its mineral wealth. Most of these deaths have definite causes: either active, when they are inflicted by institutions or authorities, or passive, when many of these tragedies are not prevented, even though they could have been. This is why it is right to speak of victimizers.

A world of compassion. There are people who, faced with the victims, react and defend them in various ways – solidarity movements, human rights movements, anti-globalization protests – and sometimes do so to the very end. Then these people are also violently deprived of their lives. Compassion leads to the greater love. Sometimes death comes through bearing a witness of commitment and love, as was the case with the Trappist monks in Algeria. There are also those who inflict death on themselves in pursuit of a liberation struggle, such as the Buddhist monks in Vietnam, or who commit suicide in order to kill their oppressors, with the aim of liberating the oppressed and in the expectation of reward in the next life. Taking a very broad analogy, all these fall under the heading of *compassion*, though the case of suicide bombers can obviously not be condoned.

Finally, there are also deaths (produced by physical or psychological torture) for fidelity to a faith, a religion, or a church, such as have been traditional throughout history and have been seen in our times in the former socialist countries, for example. These are deaths undergone *in the course of witnessing to faith*. This is the usual and the canonical understanding of martyrdom, which I am not going to examine here, since it is not what is generally happening in churches today.

One last clarification: cultures and religions usually confer 'dignity' and 'excellence' on those who die on account of their compassion (or of their fidelity in witness). Although the name is what matters least, they are called 'martyrs', 'fallen', 'heroes'. Yet the same does not happen with the masses of victims of barbarism, who are generally left nameless. I shall go into this further.

II. The 'sign of the times': death inflicted on the majorities in the Third World

In our time, 'martyrdom' has, then, taken on a new form. Many men and women have suffered violent deaths not on account of their witness to faith but because of the compassion that stems from their faith. In the church, these have been bishops and sisters, catechists and delegates of the word; in civil society, they have ranged from peasants and indigenous inhabitants to students, lawyers, and journalists. In one way and another, they have unmasked the lie used to cover over the death of the poor and have struggled against injustice. They have been people of compassion against cruelty.

But I have said that there is another more pressing development. Hundreds of thousands of human beings, often women, children, and old people, innocent and defenceless, have been slaughtered in huge massacres, without even the possibility of fleeing. In Latin America we have seen the massacres of peasant communities at El Mozote and of indigenous people in Quiché. In Africa, the genocide in Rwanda, the millions of refugees living in sub-human conditions, and the permanent destitution that brings death.

Another new development is that in Latin America most of the victimizers are Christians: oligarchs, government ministers, army officers. And the authorities that deal death have mostly been created and are largely supported by a West that calls itself democratic and – sometimes – Christian.

This new historical situation is what, in itself, forces us to rethink 'martyrdom'; in earlier times and in other places, martyrs did not 'die like that'. Vatican II also forces us to rethink it. What it says of the 'signs of the times' certainly applies to martyrdom in the Third World. This is, without a doubt, a sign of the times that I have called 'historical-pastoral': a clear expression of the 'often dramatic characteristics' (GS 4) of the world in which we live. It is also a sign of the times in the 'historical-theologal' sense: 'authentic signs of God's presence and purpose' (GS 11).

This is how it has been seen in the Third World. In 1981 Ignacio Ellacuría wrote that the principal sign of the times is always 'the people crucified in history', in which God makes his presence known. This proposition is unarguable, but it is basic. *Historically* it is self-evident; *theologally* it can only be discerned, but this is what has happened.

III. The semantic problem

Before going any further, we need to analyse the semantic problem: what, as Christians, to call the individual victims and the mass victims of today, it being the case that we have not had adequate concepts to describe this new situation. To describe the individual victims we have made *novel* use of the traditional term 'martyr'. And to describe the deaths of the masses we have *creatively* re-engaged with a concept also deriving from the biblical-Christian tradition but almost ignored: the *servant*.

With regard to the first term, the people immediately called those murdered for upholding justice 'martyrs'. Bishop Pedro Casaldáliga called Archbishop Romero 'our pastor and martyr' from the moment of his death. He actually did the same while he was still alive: 'For me those who are true martyrs in the popular sense . . . are true men who have gone to dangerous areas, where the White Warrior Union threatens, where someone can be pointed out and eventually killed as they killed Christ' (Homily of 23 Sept. 1977). All such men saw 'martyrdom' in the greater love.

With regard to the second, there has been even greater creativity, in a manner I believe to be still unknown. Neither society nor the church had any name for those massacred violently (or forced into a lingering death) that could explicitly describe the excellence and dignity of their deaths: comparing them to the 'Holy Innocents' is a confession of not knowing what to call them and indeed of little interest in them. Romero gave them a name: 'the pierced Christ'. Ellacuría called them 'the crucified people', and Casaldáliga, faced with the disappearance of whole indigenous tribes in Brazil, calls these 'crucified Indians'. This name is outstanding – even more so than that of 'martyr' – since it shows that the victims are re-creating the reality of Jesus today.

Another outstanding name has, however, also been applied to them: that of the 'suffering servant of Yahweh'. As Ellacuría said, 'This crucified people is the historical continuation of the servant of Yahweh, whom the sin of the world continues to deprive of any human features, whom the powers of this world continue stripping of everything, wresting his life from him as long as he lives.' And Archbishop Romero rejoiced that 'scriptural exegetes cannot determine whether the servant of Yahweh proclaimed by Isaiah is the suffering people or Christ come to redeem us' (Homily of 21 Sept. 1979). And it is worth pointing out that the servant is the beloved Son. The innumerable dead through repression, disappearance, massacres, hunger, destitution, now at least have a name, and this name expresses the love God has for them. This is no small matter. In my view, this is where we make the qualitative leap needed for 'rethinking martyrdom'.

IV. Individual martyrs – 'Jesus martyrs'

Those men and women who have given their lives out of reactive compassion for the victims recall Jesus. They have loved and defended the poor in life, as Puebla says that God himself does (n. 1142), and they have done so to the end, to death, and without making use of violence. And let me say that the qualification 'have defended them' is essential for understanding martyrdom today, since simply loving them through works of charity, for example, without defending them from the executioners, does not generally lead to confrontation but can sometimes even earn plaudits and admiration. So let me now venture some thoughts:

1. In the way deaths come about in the Third World today, martyrs are above all those who die like Jesus because their lives, words, and praxis have been essentially – allowing, of course, for matters of degree – like those of Jesus. They suffer a violent death for being like Jesus. This is why I call them 'Jesus martys'.

2. In this case, Jesus martyrs are not, strictly speaking, those who die *for* Christ or *because of* Christ, but those who die *like* Jesus and *for the cause of* Jesus. Their martyrdom does not result from fidelity to some mandate (which could, hypothetically, be arbitrary) of Jesus', or even from a desire for mystical identification with the crucified Jesus, but arises out of their effective following of Jesus. The essential of this martyrdom is its *affinity* with the life and death of Jesus – which does not mean that those who die for confessing their faith are not 'martyrs': they often are in an inspiring fashion.

3. Jesus is 'a witness'; his mission is to 'testify to the truth' (John 18.37), but the logic of his life and his praxis shows him still more of a 'prophet' against oppressors, and, even more than a prophet, a 'bearer of good news' and 'defender' of the poor. In judicial language, Jesus bears witness – is *martyr* – to God's love, which is partial and gratuitous to the poor. But he bears this witness through putting his love and love of the poor into practice. In this sense, I believe that to deal adequately with the 'Jesus martyrs' we need to speak not of witnesses to the truth but – still in judicial terms – of 'defenders' or 'counsels for the defence' of the poor. Jesus died for being a good shepherd who looks after his sheep, not abandoning them like a hireling, and he gave his life in their defence.

4. This martyrdom is produced not out of *odium fidei* but out of *odium iustitiae*, or – more deeply and extensively – *odium misercordiae*, hatred for a mercy that that defines the deepest nature of Jesus and his God, described by Luke as being 'moved to compassion'. This is martyrdom in the line of John's 'greater love'.

5. These martyrs can be martyrs *in* the church, but they are not martyrs *of* the church. Compassion is a basic constituent of human nature and as such can be exercised inside and outside the church. When Archbishop Romero

was assassinated at his altar, we had to go back to the twelfth century to find a precedent, in the murder of Thomas Becket, archbishop of Canterbury, but there was this difference: Thomas was killed for defending the rights, legitimate or otherwise, *of the church*, whereas Romero was killed for placing himself *on the side of the poor*. The Jesus martyrs are martyrs of humanity. figures such as Romero or Gandhi are venerated and loved around the world, in churches and religions and beyond them.

6. The reasons for giving preference to this theological concept of martyrdom are not only historical – that is how things are – but theological: Jesus Christ is 'the original sacrament of martyrdom' (Leonardo Boff), which may seem obvious but has not been so. And so by thus essentially relating the Jesus martyrs to the reality of Jesus Christ, to his life and his death, they too become *ipso facto* a central reality for faith, for the church, and for theology, with a centrality that is not very much considered, since the subject of martyrdom is studied only very marginally. The Jesus martyrs are, nevertheless, a hermeneutical principle, a mystagogy, for understanding the martyrdom of Jesus.

V. The 'crucified people'

Moving from *odium fidei* to *odium iustitiae* is a major step in rethinking martyrdom, but, in my view, it is still not the essential step from a *theologal* perspective. This consists – as I have already said – in giving a name, 'titles of respect', to the masses who suffer and die in various ways. They are the 'crucified people', the 'suffering servant of Yahweh'.

These are not mere rhetorical words. Suffice to compare the masses who barely survive and die in want, in massacres, in refugee camps, with no resources to combat AIDS, the deformed and infirm too, as the article by Carlos Mesters recalls, with the fourth song of the servant in Isaiah 52.13–53.12. The crucified people are 'a man of suffering and acquainted with infirmity' (53.3) in the deprivation of their daily lives; they are despised, left 'beyond human semblance' (52.14), without 'form or majesty' (53.2) by torture; they leave many 'astonished at him – so marred was his appearance' (52.14); they are people from whom 'others hide their faces' (53.3) because they inspire disgust and so as not to disturb their world of abundance. 'Despised and . . . held of no account' (53.3), they are also seen as 'struck down by God' (53.4), 'numbered with the transgressors' (53.12). Their suffering induces horror, contempt, dismissal, insult, denial even of their religious feelings. . .

What is said of the servant, that 'they made his grave with the wicked' (53.9) is also true today, though in our days those who have disappeared and the corpses tossed on to rubbish dumps or into secret mass graves do not even have a tomb and an epitaph. 'He did not open his mouth, like a lamb that is led to the slaughter' (53.7), just as the vast majority of those who die in massacres do not open theirs; 'By a perversion of justice he was taken away' (53.8), just as happens to those slaughtered with no defence or protection.

Finally the servant is said to be innocent: 'he had done no violence and there was no deceit in his mouth' (53.9). This is still true today: What crime had the indigenous Guatemalans burned alive in the church of St Francis in Huehuetenango committed, or the peasants assassinated in El Mozote, or the starving and dying children of Africa? This provides the starting point for some reflections.

1. By giving a biblical and Christian name to these masses of people, the main aim is to prevent a monumental scandal: the silence that closes over them in our world and the snub – to put it mildly – offered to God by ignoring his favoured creatures. Most of the US 'fallen' in Vietnam have names, which are even engraved on monuments. And something similar will be done for the victims of 11 September 2001 in New York. '9/11' is recognized everywhere: New York has a calendar. But 7 October, the day the bombing of Afghanistan began, is not: poor countries have no calendars. The victims of this have remained nameless because they are not 'wealthy', because they are 'poor'.

2. Calling these masses 'crucified people' and 'suffering servant of Yahweh' is an act of reparation that should have taken place a long time ago. And it is also an act of faith. It means not only conferring 'dignity' on the dead but seeing a saving power in them: they summon to conversion, bring light and salvation, as theologians of the Third World have realized – Ellacuría in Latin America, Pieris in Asia, and Veng in Africa.

3. Finally, the crucified people have a strictly *theo-logal* potential. They give shape to faith in a God of the weak, because they themselves are weak. This God may be accepted or not, but if this God is accepted, the crucified peoples are the most suitable setting for faith in this God. And if this God is accepted, then there is also no way out of using, in one form or another, the language of a 'crucified God': God was not only at one point on Jesus' cross reconciling the world but is still present in the crosses of history.

Furthermore, the crucified people keep the question of theodicy alive, and in a more acute form than that in which it was posed by Epicurus or

Voltaire, who were arguing from reason. This is that in faith we say that God loves the crucified people with special tenderness, yet in history God does – or can do – nothing for them. By keeping this question alive, the crucified people oblige us to take the reality of God seriously, questioning God if necessary, which is the question of theodicy. But in doing so they force us also to take the reality of our world seriously.

VI. What is the analogatum princeps of martyrdom?

We have examined two forms of death, that of the Jesus martyrs and that of the crucified people. We now need to ask, if the language will be allowed, which of the two is 'more' martyr. There are similarities between both deaths, but there are also irreconcilable differences. And I ask in which of them do we find the *analogatum princeps* of what it means to die innocently and violently at the hands of executioners. The question is not merely academic, and, obviously, it does not allow of a merely nominalist reply.

Comparing the deaths of the crucified people with that of the Jesus martyrs and even with that of Jesus, the former reflect the praxis of defence of the poor and the active struggle against the anti-kingdom *less*, and they reflect fidelity in the midst of persecution and freedom in facing death *less*, since they hardly ever have the possibility of avoiding it. On the other hand, they express historical innocence *more*, since they have done nothing (such as acrimonious prophetic denunciation, for example) to 'deserve' death, other than to be poor, and they express defencelessness *more*, since, as I have said, they have not had even the physical possibility of avoiding death. And above all they are a *better* expression of the fact that these masses of people are those who are unjustly burdened with a sin that has gradually destroyed them in life and has finally annihilated them in death.

This being said, what matters is not answering the question raised earlier, since either of these two deaths can be the *analogatum princeps* of its kind. What matters is insisting that there are *two basic types* of unjust violent death, both of supreme historical importance and supreme Christian excellence. More specifically, what matters is not forgetting the vast suffering of the world, in all its forms, and above all not ignoring the massive suffering of the poor majorities, who by being deprived of a name are stripped not only of dignity but of their very existence.

These majorities, oppressed in life and massacred in death, are those who best express the vast suffering of the world. Without intending to, without wanting to and without knowing, they 'complete in their flesh what is lacking in the passion of Christ'. And they are – whether they are called 'martyrs' or not – those human beings on whom God looks with infinite tenderness in their suffering, even before considering their personal or moral situation (Puebla n. 1142) – though they often have the basic holiness of living and laying down their lives so that all the poor may be reached by just a little life. Nevertheless, over them there descends an inhuman and anti-Christian silence, while the great ones of this world, including the saints, are exalted – 'elitistly', if I may be allowed the word – in a way that a Francis of Assisi or a Romero of America would be the first to condemn.

Rethinking the martyrdom of individuals is necessary, but it is not enough without thinking of them in conjunction with the martyred masses. And it is dangerous if, through concentrating on martyrs recognized as exceptional, we abandon the crucified people to their fate. Rethinking martyrdom ultimately means rethinking our world, asking ourselves whether the cries of the crucified people have reached us and whether the Jesus martyrs move us to compassion.

Translated by Paul Burns

Martyrdom in an Asian Struggle for Life and Dignity: Tamils in Sri Lanka

S. J. EMMANUEL

Karl Rahner on the eve of his death rightly called for an enlargement of the concept of martyrdom in the context of active struggles for truth, justice and peace in the world.[1] This call is increasingly justified in the context of the many struggles for life and dignity going on within Asia. Though this continent of peoples is blessed with great religions, cultures and traditions, human life is still threatened by many man-made practices of social injustices, discriminations, oppressions, violence and war. While the governments and their leaders in these countries may enjoy recognition in the international community and their counterparts of the first world, much of the Asian population as such still faces many threats to life and human dignity from their own governments. Hence the birth and growth of many struggles of people against their own governments for survival, human dignity and liberation.

Millions of Asians are already victims of these struggles and many face the threat of falling victims. They fight against threats to life and dignity. They die in defence of the good values of their ancestors, in defence of their birthrights, in defence of their land and heritage to them as a people. But the victims and heroes of these struggles are not recognized in history. Until and unless the victims and heroes of these struggles are recognized and their cries of agony and defence are heard by those in power, we cannot hope for a truly secure and dignified life for the human family.

It is with this interest we look into one of the longest struggles of Asia – the struggle the Tamils are waging for life and dignity on the island of Sri Lanka[2] – and look into some new images of victimhood and martyrdom emerging out of this struggle.

Martyrdom in an Asian Struggle for Life and Dignity

I. The beginning of the struggle history of Tamils in Sri Lanka

1. The history

By successive migrations which began 2000 years ago, both Singhalese and Tamils from the Indian sub-continent came to occupy different parts of the island.[3] While the majority of Singhalese, who were Buddhists, settled in the south and west of the island, rich in resouces, the Tamils, who were Hindus, settled in the arid north and east of the island. Islam, as the religion of the later migrant traders from India and Christianity, as the religion of the sixteenth-century Portuguese colonizers, also found a place in the religious niches of the island.

After many south-Indian invasions and feudal wars among the Singhalese and Tamils, there emerged three kingdoms; two Singhalese kingdoms with their capitals in Kotte and in Kandy and one Tamil kingdom with its capital in Jaffna. From the beginning of the sixteenth century, the island came under three successive waves of colonialism – the Portuguese, the Dutch and the British – each ruling the island for about 150 years. The Portuguese brought Christianity with them and the Dutch, after persecuting the Catholics, introduced their Reformed Churches. When the British took full control of the island, including the kingdom of Kandy, they introduced in 1833 one centralized administration of the whole island with Colombo as capital and English as the official language of the country. Under the British, except for the so called Indian Tamil tea-estate workers brought by them for the tea plantations, people of different ethnic origins and religious affiliations enjoyed equality of rights.

Thus the island had the natural resources and the human potential to become a multi-ethnic and multi-religious island of unity in diversity, but chauvinistic politicians helped by extreme nationalists have ruined it.

2. Struggle and counter-Tamil violence

When the three waves of colonialism(Portuguese, Dutch and British) came to an end in 1948, after almost 450 years, political power went into the hands of the Sinhala majority. Overlooking the rights of the Tamils as genuine and equal citizens of the island, the Singhalese majority converted the British centralized administration into a Sinhala Buddhist administration with privileges for the Singhalese and the Buddhists but discriminations and disadvantages for the Tamils. The last fifty years has witnessed the Sinhala majority government using a majoritarian-democracy to pass laws at will and oppress an ethnic minority by taking some of their basic rights, denying their identity as a people and displacing them from their homeland by state-aided Sinhala settlements.

When three decades of non-violent protests and democratic attempts to win their basic human rights failed miserably, the Tamil people, faced with further genocidal measures, resorted to a militant struggle against the oppressive forces of the state. State terrorism led to counter Tamil terrorism and finally to a war between the state and the LTTE, which rebelled against the state in the name of the victims. The war-weapons of the state were not mere aerial bombings and artillery shelling but years of economic blockade, media blockade, rape of Tamil women, disappearances of Tamil youth[4] and wanton destruction of the ecological resources of the Tamils. To these the Tamil response was guerilla and suicide attacks on the enemy positions.

Besides the hundreds of Sinhala soldiers and Tamil militants from very poor and suffering families who were being killed, leaving behind many widows and orphans, there were hundreds of innocent Singhalese and Tamils as collateral damages of the combat. In addition, the number of Tamil victims of aerial bombing and artillery shelling of schools, churches and temples was running into many thousands. About 800,000 Tamils have fled the island for survival and an equal number are internally displaced.

The human and material loss incurred by twenty years of war, the consequent bankruptcy of the governmental coffers and above all the people's longing for peace, have finally forced both sides to a cease-fire and to begin direct talks towards a political resolution of the conflict.[5]

II. Victims and martyrs – a religious view

1. Glorifying and demonizing tendencies will not help

The martyrs and saints on one side of the conflict tend to be the enemies and demon-figures of the other. While the actions of the state-forces are seen by many extremist Singhalese as the justified actions of a democratic state defending itself against separatism and terrorism on the part of the Tamil rebels, the non-violent and democratic pleadings of the Tamils for almost thirty years have been overlooked or even ridiculed; the actions and reactions finally resorted to by the Tamil militant LTTE against state terrorism are easily labelled as mere Tamil terrorism and so the indiscriminate killing of Tamils is justified.[6] There needs to be an unbiased understanding of the struggle and a dispassionate reading of the aspirations, convictions,

Martyrdom in an Asian Struggle for Life and Dignity

motivations and mindset of the people who are struggling as victims and as self-giving (*that-kodai*) martyrs..

Many of the Tamil Christians who have been forced to live as victims under aerial bombings, artillery shelling, economic blockades and horror rapes of women and murder of innocents have been reading the Bible from the perspective of the oppressed. And this has given them the strength to suffer and hope to continue. When from these experiences they have cried out for better understanding and justice, they have been marked out as rebels and supporters of terrorism.[7]

All Tamils, be they Hindus or Christians, tend to have a common worldview which interprets their suffering in a unique manner. Their view is largely conditioned by Hindu-Saivism, the centuries old religion of the Tamils. They believe in a destiny decreed by the gods (*thali eluththu*) and in interpreting the present suffering as caused by past evil (*karma*). A form of resignation based on the above belief helps in accepting and withstanding much suffering with patience and endurance. Thus they have suffered many discriminations and humiliations, immense loss of life and property, and remained resilient, cool and calm against the provocative and inhuman actions of the state. But such a mind-set does not encourage them to fight for the alleviation or removal of suffering. On the other hand, Saivites believe in the re-incarnation of the gods in the midst of struggles as super human beings to fight against evil. They live also in the hope that leaders will be born, even with divine power, to fight for them against the triumph of evil. Hence the tendency among Tamils to attribute divinized titles to rare and heroic leaders who can liberate them from suffering.

2. Victimhood and martyrdom

As a result of this mind-set of the people, the LTTE has set up two focal commemorations, to which all Tamils are invited. One commemorates Victimhood and the other Martyrdom. On the 23 July 1983, thousands of innocent Tamils, including fifty-three Tamil prisoners in the state prison at Welikade, were literally butchered to death all over the island. This event is commemorated annually as Black July of victims. And the night of the 26–27 November is observed as the Heroes Night (*Mahaveerar Thinam*), when thousands of Tamil heroic youth who gave their lives fighting for the liberation of their people are honoured. These two events are permanent resources for the struggle. Besides these there are two other important commemorations of those who fasted to death against the cruelties of the Sri Lankan

Army and the Indian Peace Keeping Forces respectively *(Satyagrahis – Annai Poopathy and Deleepan)*.

Both Hindus and Christians participate actively in these commemorations honouring their dear ones as self-sacrificing heroes of Tamil liberation. Though the majority of the Tamils are Hindus who burn their dead, the LTTE bury those who die in combat with due military honours in war cemeteries. These cemeteries are looked upon by the people as hallowed resting places of their heroic martyrs for the cause of liberation of the Tamils.[8] Without attempting to explain away, justify or encourage violence in any form, one can easily understand how a struggling people and their leaders are forced by the oppressor and his war-machinery to react to state injustice and state terrorism through suicide bombings, even in the face of damage to innocent lives.

Repeated pleas of the Tamils not to air-drop bombs on civilian populations under the pretext of targeting terrorists went unheard for years. Air attacks were carried out even on refugee camps, churches, temples, schools and hospitals, and thousands were perishing. The Tamils had no planes or a bombs to retaliate, so what action could be expected on behalf these victims? Some suicide cadres of the LTTE secretly penetrated the military base situated next to the civil airport in Colombo, made themselves into human bombs and blew up the very jet planes which had been bombing their brethren day and night for years. That this mission was planned and executed without killing a single civilian and with the least amount of collateral damage shows the real target of those who are suffering. Such are the reactions of an oppressed Tamil people against the oppressor who blindly refuses to recognize their struggle.

III. Failure and hope

1. Failure of the church

Christians in Sri Lanka, though a minority (7%) in comparison with Buddhists (67%), Hindus (18%) and Muslims (8%), have the unique strategy of counting membership from both the majority Singhalese and from the minority Tamils. They have had a key role to play in fostering Sinhala-Tamil ethnic harmony. But by their apolitical stance and diplomatic silence, they have failed to recognize adequately both the struggle of their people for life and dignity and the heroic victims of the struggle. True, they have shown the compassion of a good Samaritan for the victims and offered humanitarian service to the victims of violence and war. But they have not shown the courageous face of Jesus, who became victim and martyr for the sake of others. Hence a deep conversion of the church is needed before it can play an active and meaningful role in bringing the conflict to an end and in building true peace in the island.

2. *Religious recognition and support for struggles*

The phenomena of victimhood and martyrdom unfolding within the liberation struggle of the Tamils, though condemned by the opponents, ridiculed by the media and abhorred by the modern society as mere terrorism, still raise disturbing but valid questions to our present day institutions, whether they are the so called 'democratic state', the neutral NGOs or the church within such a state.

The long struggles of people for life and dignity are focussing the attention of the world more and more on the new culprits of oppression and oppressive structures. The oppressors are not only the governments of the people but also the bigger and richer powers of the world outside. These major powers of the world tend to strengthen the hand of the oppressor rather than help the victims of oppression.

The Western world especially, forgetting its own struggle for liberation, proclaiming its doctrine as the one 'new world-order' and wielding great political and financial power, tends to absolutize its own interests, to manipulate human rights and international laws to suit itself, and glibly accuses struggling people of terrorism within its own definition of the word. Moreover, it heaps up weapons of destruction as 'aid' in the hands of despotic powers and bulldozes over the genuine aspirations of people who are dying for their convictions.

Struggling people, believing in the righteousness of the international community, still appeal to their highest institutions, for example to the UN and its structures. But to their disappointment they find that even these are subject to manipulations by the super powers!

Most of those who suffer and struggle are relying more and more on the cries of their victims and on the heroic martyrdom of their rebels who have given up their own lives so that others may have a just and free life. They expect from all religions more solidarity in their suffering and a courageous stance for justice in their favour.

If all religious institutions can go beyond their solidarity and humanitarian assistance to recognize more positively the struggles of people, their victims and heroes, and as religions stand up for the values at stake, then the evil powers of the world will not be able to bulldoze over the struggles of people.

Notes

1. See 'Martyrdom Today', *Concilium* 163, March 1983, p. 11.
2. Of the 70 million Tamils all over the world, over 60 million live in Tamil Nadu of India. The others are in Sri Lanka, Malaysia, Singapore, South Africa and Myanmar. The struggle we are here speaking of is about the 3.5 millions of Tamils on the island of Sri Lanka.
3. *Racial Discrimination: The Record of Sri Lanka* published by South Asian Human Rights Documentation Centre ISBN No: 81–87379-09-X; http://www.hrdc.net/sahrdc/
4. Sri Lanka has the second highest number of disappearances in the world. Only Iraq has more.
5. With the Norwegian government acting as mediators, the government of Sri Lanka and the LTTE entered into a cease-fire agreement in February 2002 and on 16 September started talks to find a just and peaceful solution to the ethnic conflict.
6. The denial of and reduction of fifty years of ethnic conflict and twenty years of war to the mere fighting of Tamil terrorists was a ploy by the state to win finance and weapons from the international community.
7. Having been at the head of an academic community of the major seminary of Jaffna for the ten years of the struggle 1986–96, I had the privilege of voicing the aspirations and sufferings of this oppressed people at various international meetings, including the UN sessions on Human Rights in Geneva.
8. For the majority of Singhalese and their government, the LTTE cadres are merely Tamil terrorists who are to be despised even after death. In December 1995, when 500,000 Tamils left the Jaffna peninsula in the face of the threat of the Sinhala Army, the latter occupied Jaffna, destroyed all monuments of commemoration in the peninsula and also bulldozed the largest war cemetery of the Tamils.

Martyrs of Latin America

ELSA TAMEZ

¡*Guatemala, nunca más!* ('Guatemala, Never Again', 1988) was the title of five thick volumes produced by the inter-diocesan process called 'Recovery of the Historical Memory' (REMHI),[1] which contain a record of the inhuman abuses and massacres that produced around 200,000 victims in Guatemala between 1977 and 1996. The report on abuses of human rights in Brazil is similarly called 'Brazil, Never Again', and there are also 'Argentina, Never Again' and 'Uruguay, Never Again'. The statement 'never again' is above all a declaration of faith and hope, since in the current situation of Latin America, martyrs are still appearing. Brazil's 'never more' was followed a year later by the murder of Fr Joshimo, campaigner for landless peasants, and Guatemala's own 'never more' was followed by the assassination of Archbishop Juan José Gerardi Conedera, just two days after the report on the abuses had been published. By the brutality of the murder, in which his head was crushed, the assassins were trying to 'un-write' the book, to put an end to the memory of the martyrs by making another martyr after the appearance of the first edition of the REMHI report, as though ironically declaring 'Guatemala, Ever Again'.

These 'never again' reports from Latin America do not belong to the past. 'Never again' is a statement issued permanently in the intense desire that one day it will become reality. Because, with the commitment we Christians have to human rights for human beings, there will always be more and more volumes to recover the memory of those who have been martyred. The purpose of this brief article is to put forward something of the reality of martyrdom in Latin America. I have chosen Guatemala because of my closeness to that country and because the REMHI report divulges practically all the information possible. I have, though, brought in some names of martyrs from other countries to show how similar other cases are.

I. The background to martyrdom and martyrs

In Latin America it is not affirmation of 'doctrinal truths' or abstract and unhistorical theological beliefs that leads to martyrdom. It is the witness of the faithful, lay people, catechists, religious Brothers and Sisters, priests and bishops reflected in their works of justice on behalf of the poor: landless peasants, families without water or other basic resources, underpaid and exploited industrial and agricultural workers, indigenous victims of discrimination. Underlying everything is the situation of injustice. This emerges from the testimonies of numerous martyrs and survivors, such as the following: 'What happened in the violence from the beginning was the injustice in which few had a living wage and very many a starvation wage, in my view, and from there came these groups in defence of the people among whom there were tremendous massacres, in which anyone who wanted to help with what was wrong was eliminated with no turn to to ask for justice, because no one was prepared to speak out.'[2] The author of this statement, given in its original simple words, is referring to the period of greatest repression by the army in Guatemala (1981–83), when the victims of kidnap, torture, and murder included several priests. Among these were Faustino Villanueva, shot with a pistol in his parish office; Fr Juan Alonso Fernández, machine-gunned in a ravine; and Fr Fr José María Gran Cirera, machine-gunned on a lonely path.[3] These priests, like the majority of the murdered and 'disappeared', were simply part of the poor and indigenous communities, trying to protect them against the arbitrary acts of the army and the landowners. The liturgies celebrated in their honour were true liturgies for martyrs.

This picture was repeated in other countries: Fr Álvaro Ulcue Chocue and the Lauritas Sisters in Colombia were persecuted by the army, supported by the landowners. The indigenous mayor of Torobio sent a message to the archbishop, defending his parish priest, Álvaro, in which he wrote: 'The rich do not understand us in this change we have initiated and this is why they hate him . . . they calumniate Father as a communist, as a subversive, and even call him a murderer, but it is because they do not understand the Light of the Gospel. On 10 November 1984, as he was preparing to carry out a baptism, two unknown men – later identified as Miguel Ángel and Orlando Río, policemen – shot him from a motorbike. Fr Álvaro had written to President Betancur, saying, 'If only you knew what it is like to "live" in the midst of hunger, insecurity (murders, kidnaps, flattening of houses, propagation of ideological interests that confuse the native people, abuse of women), lack of housing, health, education and basic necessities . . . If we are silent they crush us, if we protest they call us subversives . . .'[4]

Martyrs of Latin America

The list of martyrs also includes many women, such as Teresita Ramírez, of the Company of Mary, in Cristales, Colombia, who decided to support the peasants in their struggle for light, electricity, education and health care in their region, even asking for parish priests to be nominated, since these scarcely ever arrived; in May 1988 she was killed by having her clothes set on fire as she came out from the hall in which she taught. And there are many others like her, religious as well as laywomen such as the Guatemalans Dora Azmitia, a youth leader who was kidnapped; María Ramírez, a catechist murdered during the massacre that took place at the Spanish Embassy in Guatemala on 31 March 1980;[5] and Ligia Martínez, who worked alongside the poor in rural and peripheral areas of Guatemala, murdered on 3 October 1981.[6] The case of the four Maryknoll Sisters raped and murdered in El Salvador in 1982 is well known.

It would be impossible to name all the martyrs of Latin America, men and women, in this short account. I have mentioned just a few names, typical of the thousands kidnapped and murdered and virtually all countries of Latin America. They were decent Christian people, clerics, religious, lay, men and women, who were trying to put the gospel of Jesus Christ into practice by defending the rights of the poor and excluded, for which they were persecuted, seized, made to disappear or murdered with complete impunity, since those responsible were usually the military, paramilitary or other state forces.[7] It is important for local communities and nations to know the names of the martyrs, including their family names, since this helps to keep them alive in people's memories and makes them present in the hope of 'never more'. This is why volume IV of the REMHI report lists virtually all the names of the 52,429 victims documented.

II. Martyr peoples

In Latin America we talk not only of individual martyrs but also of martyr peoples. In the liturgies celebrated for victims there is always a time dedicated to evoking those who gave their lives for the well-being of their brothers and sisters in the community in which they served. Their names are read out loud and their lives and deaths recalled, as an offering to the community and to God. Not because they have made a suicidal sacrifice, but because their commitment to Kingdom values clashed with the values of businessmen and landowners. Names of priests, of female and male religious, are read out, as well as those of delegates of the word, catechists, and Protestant pastors, such as Santos Jiménez y Jerónimo (known as Don Chono);[8] those of Mayan priests, such as Fr Venancio Ramírez, are also pronounced, as well as those of lay men and women, little known, but who collaborated in community work and risked their lives out of love of their neighbours. One case that has become internationally known is that of the anthropologist Mirna Mack Chang, murdered in Guatemala on 11 September 1990 for obtaining information about people who had been displaced. Besides those internationally-known names such as Archbishop Romero and the Jesuit priests of El Salvador, the list of unknown martyr's names is endless.

In Latin America, according to Jon Sobrino, a martyr is someone who reproduces the death of Jesus, since the essential aspect of martyrdom is affinity with the death of Jesus, and in this sense, the martyrs are those who defend some central aspect of the Kingdom of God.[9] Many witness statements make explicit reference to the death of Jesus. This is one such: 'What we have seen was terrible, burned bodies, women impaled on wooden stakes as thought they were animals to be roasted on a spit, all bent double, and children murdered and hacked about with machetes. Women also *killed like Christ*.[10] 'Killed like Christ' meaning simply because the army saw the people as dangerous. In the words of one witness, Alta Verapaz, 'The soldiers had now begun to kill; not a word was spoken; they were not asking if anyone was guilty or not; that day they were killing.'[11]

These two accounts refer to two of the 422 massacres recorded in the REMHI report. Most of the so-called 'scorched earth' massacres in the towns and villages of Quiché, Huehuetenango, and other regions followed the counter-insurgency strategy known as 'fish out of water'. Officialdom saw guerrillas as fish and their communities as water: the latter had to disappear so as to leave the guerrillas with no support and nowhere to go. This is why there were massive slaughters of men, women, old people, and children. Nothing was left alive, houses were burned, and crops destroyed.

So now we are asking if such people were martyrs. Clearly, children do not die for bearing witness through their work for justice and defence of the poor. They are killed arbitrarily through the cruelty of counter-insurgency measures – like the children who died in the massacre at Cuarto Pueblo (March 1982), who were thrown on to heaps in the hall of the health centre to be burned alive.[12] The same can be said of many of the old people and the young ones, men and women. Plundered, raped, tortured, humiliated, killed and thrown into ditches, these people suffered such fates inflicted with total gratuitousness. This is why those who tell of such events relate them to the death of Christ, even though they may have no idea of a cause and even though they are not strictly recognized as martyrs by the church. 'The church declares to be martyrs those who suffer violent death at the hands of any persecutor who is acting out of hatred of faith in Christ or of any virtue related to God.'[13] In this sense such victims may well be martyrs, even though the disposition required of the victim may not be present, since the church requires 'that there be a readiness on the part of victims to accept death out of commitment to their faith'.[14] In these massacres, some may have understood 'this disposition', but most will not have done. People do not want to die, nor do they accept death, because they know that God does not want them to die; this is what they have learned in their Christian communities. So in a certain sense they do not want to be martyrs. But we look on many Christians as martyrs because such victims, such as Celina and Alba Ramírez, the two ordinary women who died with the Jesuits murdered in the university of San Salvador in November 1989, show with extreme clarity the wickedness and sin of the world that vents its anger on Christian prophets and also on innocent people. The blood of the martyrs is mingled with the blood of these victims and this mingled blood is what makes the blood of Jesus Christ present in the world today.

III. An end to prophets and martyrs in the third millennium?

No one wants martyrs; the church does not, and neither does God. Nevertheless, in contexts of poverty, oppression, and repression martyrs are a sign that Christian communities are marching and declaring themselves against oppressive and violent regimes. There are no dictatorships left today, but oppression and poverty have deepened, and military violence, as in Colombia, and criminal violence, as in all countries, have increased. At the present time a sort of truce is in operation, but it will not be a lasting one, since the number of children dying of starvation is reaching intolerable levels, lack of work and lack of food are beyond what patience can bear, and this, unlike the ideological struggles of previous years, is becoming tremendously subversive. Cardinal Oscar Rodríguez Maradiaga of Honduras certainly thinks so: in an interview dealing with external debt and corruption in Central America he said, 'We are touching bottom, and the worst is that no one wants to see that we are facing the greatest subversion of all time, the subversion of poverty, which is very different from the ideological struggles that cost thousands of lives in the 1960s and 1970s.'[15]

It is important to take stock of the situation today, because recovery of the memory of the martyrs and all violations of human rights is essential not only for 'repairing the social fabric' of societies such as that of Guatemala or just for preventing a repetition of the violations; recovery of the memory of the martyrs is vital for us today because their memory can help us to recover the sensitivity and solidarity we have lost thanks to the consumer society created by the present globalized free-market system.

The struggle for justice is not something that belongs in the past. 'Never more' is still a statement of lasting faith, even if more volumes have to be written to take account of the number of victims who are being left out. Injustices and impunity are still in force, as proved by the fact that the day I wrote this article, 4 October 2002, the Fourth Court of Appeal in Guatemala absolved those who had been condemned to thirty years imprisonment for the murder of Archbishop Gerardi.[16] This was a major blow delivered by the legal system. As the present archbishop riposted when he heard the verdict absolving the murderers: 'Justice should be done. It is not as though they killed a dog.'

While people lack the right to be human, martyrs and prophets will continue to show their presence in Latin America.

Translated by Paul Burns

Notes

1. Compiled and published by the Human Rights Office of the Archdiocese of Guatemala, directed by Mgr Juan Gerardi, Guatemala 1998.
2. Case 3877, Santa Cruz del Quiché, Quiché 1981.
3. See *Y dieron la vida por El Quiché . . .*, publication sponsored by OSM-CONFRAGUA and Days for Life and Peace, Guatemala 1992.
4. *Aquellas muertes que hicieron resplandecer la vida*, Bogotá 1992, p. 113. The book relates the martyrdom of twenty-four people, most of whom were assassinated by the army or paramilitaries.
5. The embassy was burned, and thirty-nine people died in it, most of them peasants from the Quiché region.
6. See *Mártires de Guatemala*, Guatema, CONFREGUA 1998.
7. According to the Guatemala report, the government forces were responsible for 87.65% and the guerrillas for 4.81%. REMHI vol. IV, p. 488.
8. Assassinated on 19 November 1980.
9. Cited by A. E. Román López, *Martiriología, profetismo y esperanza en América Latina*, thesis from the Latin American Biblical University 2001, p. 43.
10. Case 9839, Cuarto Pueblo, Ixcán, Quiché 1985 (my italics).
11. Case 6629, Cobán 1980.
12. See R. Falla, *Masacres de la selva, Ixcán, Guatemala (1975–1982)*, Editorial Universitaria 1992, p. 100.

13. See *Monseñor Juan Gerardi, testigo fiel de Dios*, Guatemala, Bishops' Conference 1999, p. 219.
14. Ibid.
15. See *La Nación*, Sunday 6 October 2002, 22A.
16. Retired Colonel Lima Estrada, Captain Byron Lima Oliva, and Sergeant José Obdulio Villanueva, together with Fr Mario Orantes, the dead bishop's secretary, an accomplice of the soldiers, had been condemned to twenty years in prison.

Africa, A Martyred Continent: Seed of a New Humanity

TERESA OKURE, SHCJ

In the traditional sense Africa has been a continent of martyrs since the beginning of Christianity. Among them were Perpetua, a noble lady of 22 years, and Felicity, her pregnant maid-servant, both of Carthage, martyred at the amphitheatre (*c.* AD 203). Cyprian, also of Carthage, was killed under the Emperor Valerian (*c.* AD 258). Most modern African saints are martyrs in the traditional sense: Clementine Anuarite of Zaire, beaten to death by soldiers at the order of the Colonel of Simba for refusing to break her vow of virginity; Blessed Isidore Bakanja of Zaire (former Belgian Congo) also beaten to death, bathed in a pool of blood after receiving some 250 strokes by a *mzungu* (Swahili for 'a white man'), for refusing to stop saying his prayers and wearing the scapular; the martyrs of Mombasa (African men, women and children, led mainly by women, martyred with some Portuguese in August 1631, for being Christians, by a Muslim whom the missionaries had once 'converted' to Christianity, educated and placed as ruler over the people) . . .

Frederick Quinn's *African Saints and Martyrs* lists martyrs whose reasons for martyrdom cuts across boundaries of religion, race, class and sex. Manche Masemola (1913–28) was killed for her faith by her non-Christian parents. Bernard Mizeki (1861–1906), a catechist of Mozambican origin, was killed in Cape Town during the Mashona rebellion in 1896. He was suspected as an agent of European imperialism. Others from South Africa listed by Quinn were killed by Christians of the apartheid regime. They include Stephen Biko (1946–77), a well-known political activist; Valiamma Munusay, a teenage Hindu young woman, follower of Mohandas Ghandi (1897–1914), who died in jail where she was sent as a passive resister, and Imam Abdullah Haron (1924–69), an Islamic leader, murdered by the South African police. To this list one would add Hector Peterson, the young lad shot dead by the South African police in Soweto during the students' uprising against the enforced Bantu education.

Africa, A Martyred Continent: Seed of a New Humanity 39

Outside South Africa, in Zaire Simon Kimbangu (*c.* 1889–1951), founder of the Kimbanguist Church, died in jail where he was imprisoned by 'orthodox' Christians, after enduring thirty years of solitary confinement in Elizabethville, Belgian Congo. His martyrdom was followed by that of an estimated 150,000 of his followers. More recently, the martyrs of the Christian Fraternity in Buta, Burundi, including some forty young seminarians, in 1997 were killed in an attack alleged to be by a Hutu army, as a spillover of the genocide in Rwanda. In Nigeria, one would add the many Christians who have been killed by Muslim fanatics over the past two decades, the latest onslaught arising from the protest against Nigeria's hosting of the Miss World pageant in November-December 2002. This list is by no means exhaustive, but it does show that from the beginning of Christianity until now Africa has not lacked martyrs as they are traditionally understood, whether they are canonized or not.

I. A martyred continent

In the context of 'rethinking martyrdom', this study invites us to review Africa as a martyred continent. If Africa is a 'martyred continent', how and by whom has she been martyred? What are the nature and content of her witness? To and for whom has she borne this ultimate witness? How can Africa's martyrdom be the seed of or give birth to a new humanity?

The above questions about Africa's martyrdom can be answered comprehensively thus: Africa's martyrdom lies in the very fact of her existence. Africa is and has been martyred because of her God-given reality as a race distinct from other races (though in reality there is only one human race). Africa has been and is still being martyred because the languages, cultures and skin colour of her children differ from those of other peoples. She has been martyred because of her God-given wealth in people, rich natural and mineral resources, fauna, forestry. She has been martyred for her history, sculpture, hospitality, religion and a culture that in its rich diversity combines religion and politics (church and state, to use the traditional expression) as one integrated way of life. Africa was martyred in the past by slave traders, colonialists, neo-colonialists, apartheid lords who in diverse ways despoiled her of her multifaceted wealth. European countries used her as strategic locations for conducting their cold war away from their borders and left her decimated by internal wars and strife, littered with broken tanks and explosive land minds. She has been martyred by technologically developed nations who see her as a ready-made source of cheap labour and raw materials for their industries and survival, and who continue to see her as a convenient market for dumping all kinds of used and outmoded commodities. Africa has been martyred by powerful Western nations who set up and support military despots all over Africa so they can freely loot her rich resources (gold, oil, silver, copper, diamond, etc.) in collaboration with their stooges. In the history of the human race, Africa has been martyred because she has been denied her status as the cradle of humanity, of civilization. Her geographical location as the womb of the earth has counted for nothing.

This martyrdom which started from the moment of the Europeans' contact with Africa in the late sixteenth century continues in diverse ways and forms to the present. The current plight of the continent, tagged the forgotten continent, yet very much in the news media as the icon of all that is bad, is the fruit of these past martyrdoms, be they economic poverty, bad government, militarism, corruption, refugee problems, human trafficking, ethnic clashes, the spread of pandemic, communicable diseases (such as HIV/AIDS) and the tendency of leaders always to look to the West for approval and support in all undertakings. Briefly, Africa has been martyred anthropologically, historically, socio-culturally, economically, politically and for its religion. An abundance of studies, including recent investigations, document it. Lack of space prevent us from even listing the literature. For practical reasons we will elucidate just a few of these points, though they are all intertwined.

1. Ontological martyrdom

Race and sex are ontological by nature, gifts of God inherited by birth. Differing from nationality, race carries with it the notion of culture, language and world-view. Class is not essentially ontological, for some are born great while others can have greatness bestowed on them. In Africa, stately kings and majestic queens born great (like the Zulu Kings in South Africa) had their greatness taken away from them as those who martyred their continent reduced them and their people to servitude. This type of martyrdom, 'anthropological impoverishment', needs little explanation. Briefly, in the past (and in some instances even now), Black Africans have been denied full humanity and called all kinds of names: 'baboon on two legs gifted with speech', bush, savage, primitive, pagan and uncivilized. Africa's religion has been tagged fetish, animist. These labellings and others remain deeply alive in the minds of many Westerners and influence their perception of Africans; they also affect the self-perception of many Africans themselves.

Africa, A Martyred Continent: Seed of a New Humanity

With efforts to deny that Black Africans are truly human beings have gone systematic attempts to falsify Africa's history by denying that ancient Egypt, Nubia-Sudan and Ethiopia, to which the world owes its civilization, were peopled by Blacks; or if by Blacks, that this Africa was indeed the cradle of civilization. Cheikh Anta Diop, who has conducted a comprehensive survey of these efforts, views them as attempts 'to whiten Black Africa'. Today the effort continues in the alleged plan to excise northern Africa from the rest of the continent and incorporate it into the European Union. The myth of 'sub-Saharan Africa', said to be also the region 'north of the Limpopo', is part of this debilitating agenda. Its effect is to decimate and weaken Africa continentally and geographically, and make her bleed still further. All this is in addition to the deep and localized wounds inflicted upon her when she was carved and parcelled out for European nations at the Berlin Conference.

Why was Africa's martyrdom seen as beneficial to Europeans during the slave trade era? Because the prosperity and very survival of 'the new world' of the Whites depended on the martyrdom of Africa. To effect this martyrdom with a clean conscience, it became necessary to project Africans as subhuman, people who were devoid of intelligence, culture, humanity and even a soul. With this false projection firmly in place, it was then easy for people who regarded themselves as Christians to capture, buy and export Africans to serve as beasts of burden in their plantations.

That Africans were denied intelligence or said at best to be of low intelligence justified the poor quality education that was given to them (reading, writing and arithmetic, not maths), an education which equipped them to be of service as junior clerks to the colonial masters, not to themselves. White South Africans gave the Blacks inferior education to ensure that they did not rise up to challenge the Whites. King Leopold of Belgium specifically instructed his missionaries to ensure that they gave the Blacks of the Democratic Republic of Congo no education that would empower them to rise up and oppose his own efforts to possess their land and loot their cultural heritage.

To theologically justify the evil practice, Western theologians developed the theory of 'the curse of Ham', namely, that by enslaving the Blacks and entrenching the equally evil apartheid system in South Africa, they were merely carrying out God's justifiable curse of the Blacks, descendants of Ham. Hitler used a similar theology later to justify the holocaust of the Jews.

2. Socio-cultural, political, economic and religious martyrdom

Colonialism was accompanied by a systematic looting of Africa's great mineral and other resources: animal parts, timber, ebony, ivory, gold, diamond, copper. Africa's economic resources, deep respect for nature and the land suffered irreparable blows through this reckless looting and exploitation. The continent has yet to recover from this economic despoiling. To worsen matters, in a process that started after independence, most African currencies today have been devalued beyond measure by the policies of the International Monetary Fund and the World Bank.

By their strategy of divide and rule, the colonial masters introduced and entrenched in Africa the practice of breaking up, not only nations, but also well-established infra-structures by which the Africans governed themselves and regulated their communities in a welfare system that imaged that of the gospel. The African philosophy of life, 'I am because we are, and because we are, I am', underscores this. But the economics of selfishness took over this community-oriented economy. Martyred Africa is yet to recover from this onslaught.

This stripping of Africa was rooted in lies, the denial of the real evidence about the continent and its peoples. The European exploiters spread the lies that Africans lacked culture. Yet they looted African cultural artifacts to adorn their museums in Europe. They accused Africa of lacking morality. Yet Africans had very high moral values in the upbringing of youth, the regulation of sexual relationships, respect for life and for the land. The exploiters viewed African religions (and in some cases still view them) as animism. Yet they used African titles for God (Abasi, Chukwu, Olodumare, Nyame, Kulunkulu, etc.) to indicate the biblical God. Yet Africa gave the world the notion of monotheism, cultic religion, the priesthood and taught it to write through the activity of its priests. Africa gave the world its knowledge of science and taught it to philosophize. Having in the past condemned Africa's integrated religion and life, her respect for nature and her educational and socializing methods, the West today is making serious efforts to return to those very methods and practices. Concern for ecology and eco-spirituality are fast becoming fashionable. Africa's child-rearing techniques such as breast feeding and carrying the child on the back, once considered as bush and primitive, are now being preached as the best method to ensure healthy physique and sound emotional development of the child.

3. A living martyr

The martyrdom of Africa in diverse forms is not merely a thing of the past. The longstanding propaganda about Africa as a destitute and primitive continent continues today in covert ways. Fear of the consequences of confessing the sin and unmasking the lie leads the Western media to continue to project Africa as the home of immorality, the icon of everything that is bad, and more recently, the icon and natural habitat of HIV/AIDS. Hardly does the Western media speak of Africa without subjecting it to its morbid preoccupation with all that dehumanizes: the poorest countries of the world are said to belong to Africa.

African governments have been persuaded to devote their whole attention to combating HIV/AIDS, Western in origin, if they are to be heard by or receive a grant from the West. The economic value to the West of this project is hardly ever mentioned. Drugs for combating the killer disease are produced in the West. Even those said to be sold to Africa at a subsidized rate end up in markets in Europe at a higher rate. Thabo Mbeki's cry that world policy makers pay attention to how their policies (of a new world order) continue to kill the economic, political and human resources of Africa and see these policies as graver aspects of HIV/AIDS than the actual infection, continue to fall on deaf ears. The USA will readily give grants for combating HIV/AIDS but not for programmes that will give people a better education and humane living conditions and so eliminate HIV/AIDS and 'other sexually transmitted diseases' that the Western media loves to proclaim daily as being the lot of Africa. Has Africa a preserve of HIV/AIDS that it must spend all its energy to combat it while the rest of the world continues with its normal life? What debilitating effects has the HIV/AIDS song for Africa on its citizens? A colleague noted recently that in Uganda, for instance, the interest is no longer on how to live, but on different ways of dying.

The continuous brain drain from Africa to America and the West is yet another form of Africa's living martyrdom. In Nigeria today some ask whether the granting of lottery funds to Africans to go and work in the US is not yet another effort to reduce Africans to a new form of slavery. In many cases the scholars and technicians are attracted by the better salaries and living and working conditions offered by the West. Would Africans feel the need to migrate to the West if they had the same living conditions at home? The West blames the ineptitude and underdevelopment of African leaders for these poor conditions. But it forgets that its own colonial and neo-colonial example and policies served and continue to serve as models for these leaders. As the colonialists ruled Africa by looting and showing contempt for the people, so their African successors, persuaded that the European way of governing is the best, continue to imitate the style of these colonial masters by looting the heritage and treasuries of their nations and bequeathing them to the West. This brings them richer rewards than investing in their own countries.

The catalogue of Africa's martyrdom could go on indefinitely. The pejorative naming of Africa in the media is a way of killing her each day. For Africans words are not neutral; they effect what they say. What the Western media says about Africa furnishes a wardrobe of garments of mourning and death that Africa is forced to wear daily, like an African widow perpetually in mourning. A new way of speaking about the continent would help Africa to rise, shake off her garments of mourning and put on the royal robes and jewelry with which God has bedecked and endowed her abundantly by nature. Today the West knows that Africa is a force to reckon with, and the deep-seated fear of what a united Africa can become may be at the root of the continued subversive effort to decimate her through the media and other debilitating policies. Yet the time has come for Africa to sing a brand new song, to reject those voices which can only speak of Africa pejoratively even when they supposedly mean well. The time has come to reap the rich fruit which martyred Africa bears and offers to the world as the seed of a new humanity.

II. Hope of a new humanity

The blood of martyrs is the seed of Christianity. It fosters the growth of faith among the very people who killed the martyrs and spreads the martyrs' cause. An emerging phenomenon today, even if this is still imperceptible, is that Africa is rising in many respects from the ashes of its age-old and sustained martyrdom to reclaim its rightful, God-given place in the human family. Christ's death was followed by his resurrection. One who dies in Christ rises to new life in him. Today Africa is rising strongly and unmistakably from the dead. She is learning, however slowly, to reject the poisonous foods that have been fed to her both in the past and the present. Among the politically striking evidence of this rising from the dead are the fall of the apartheid regime in South Africa, the collapse of military regimes covertly backed by some Western countries (though the debris and the urge to stage coups still remain), and the recent New Partnership in Development

(NEPAD) forged by African heads of state (however imperfect and top heavy this project may have been in its conception).

Perhaps the greatest evidence of Africa's resurrection is the awakening of Africans themselves, their determination to speak for themselves and not simply allow the West to define and control them. African scholars, both in the motherland and in the diaspora, are digging up their past and reconnecting with their glorious history in all disciplines. They are reclaiming their cultural heritage and becoming aware of their invaluable contribution to human history and civilization. The effort is primarily a way of their telling themselves 'Yes, we are', regardless of others who may tell them 'You are not'. Africans are reclaiming not only their despised cultural heritage but also their unique role in the development of the civilization of humanity. While the world is speaking of cancelling Africa's debts, Africans themselves are calling on the West to confess the debt it owes to Africa and Africans, to make amends and thus be freed from the self-inflicted slavery caused by lies about Africa and their unquestioning acceptance by those who have never visited Africa. Pope John XXIII would call these efforts 'a sign of our times'. He would praise Africans for refusing to continue to allow themselves to be exploited and dehumanized, since he declared that 'Those who know they have rights have the responsibility to claim their rights and others have the corresponding duty to respect them as they claim those rights.'

On the Western front itself, church leaders are beginning to confess openly, however slowly and unsatisfactorily, the role of the West in the impoverishment and destruction of Africa. As part of the three-year preparation for the Great Jubilee 2000, Pope John Paul II took the bold step of asking pardon for the colonial exploitation of Africa in the past. On the Protestant side, the 1998 WCC General Assembly in Harare started a 'Journey of Hope in Africa'. The US Catholic Bishops' Conference in November 2001 issued a 'Call to Solidarity with Africa', where it acknowledges:

> Slavery, a system fundamentally evil and base, stole from the African continent many of its most precious resources: men, women, and children. Millions of people were forcibly uprooted from their families and communities to lands and conditions so alienating and dehumanizing that words cannot convey the depth of their suffering. Our own nation, as well as the rest of the Americas, still lives with the effects of this evil. Our own people still bear slavery's scars and live its history – a history that has not yet been fully acknowledged or entirely reconciled. America's own

responsibility to overcome this legacy of slavery and racism should be reflected in our domestic and international programs and policies.

Archaeology on its part is unearthing the as yet irrefutable evidence that Africa is the cradle of humanity. 'Nowhere else in the world have as many fossilized human remains been discovered as those unearthed on the continent of Africa' (Johnson, *The Mitochondrial Mother*, p. 7). If the evidence of the mitochondrial gene is correct, it means that to begin with we are all Black Africans. The celebration of Africa is truly the celebration of ourselves as a human race.

Mary Robinson, UN Commissioner for Human Rights, once remarked that the world owes a great debt to Africa for its contribution in the development of the 1948 Universal Declaration of Human Rights. This Declaration with its thirty articles was greatly inspired by Africa's struggle at home and in the diaspora to overcome slavery and other forms of racial discrimination. Here again the martyrdom of Africa has yielded a lasting resurrection, an invaluable seed for a new humanity.

Martyred Africa has indeed been and will continue to bear the seed of a new humanity. For if her martyrdom meant her death and the death of many nations fed with lies about Africa, her resurrection can mean nothing less than the birth and burgeoning forth of a new humanity where truth about our common human origin will be told, and where all will recognize and celebrate God's goodness to humanity given through Africa. The emerging truth about martyred Africa is already setting both Africa and the entire human family free. Africa has martyrs in the traditional sense; the rethinking of martyrdom for Africa entails a rethinking of human relationships and a recognition of the fundamental human rights of all peoples. This is and will remain Africa's legacy to our world community. It is all God's work, for no amount of effort to kill Africa can subject it to endless death, prevent it from rising from the dead or separate it from God's love.

II. A Critical Reinterpretation of Martyrdom in the Light of Scripture and Tradition

Jesus the Martyr

SEÁN FREYNE

The Greek verb *martyrein* and its cognates *martys* – from which our term 'martyr' is derived – and *martyria* take their primary semantic significance from the legal sphere. To bear witness is to attest solemnly to the truth of one's assertions about events or persons before a judge in a law court. However, the word-family has a wider significance than the merely forensic. It can also be used in the broader, though related, sense of making a public statement about one's personal beliefs and convictions. It was a combination of these two contexts, the public and the legal, that gave rise to the Greek term *martys* acquiring the more specialized meaning of martyr, namely one who is prepared to die for his or her beliefs by publicly acknowledging them when challenged, irrespective of the consequences. As the Christian movement began to attract the attention of the Roman civil authorities, it was increasingly seen as seditious in that its members often refused to acknowledge the emperor as a divine figure, even when put under the most severe physical pressure. Instead, many gladly accepted death joyfully, even with eagerness, believing that they would share in the crown of victory with Jesus, their crucified saviour, who himself had suffered an unjust death at the hands of Roman authorities.

I. 'Witness' in the Gospels

A brief word study of the four Gospels can assist in tracking this evolution of the term from witness in a court of law to martyr for Christ's sake. In Mark, our earliest Gospel, followed by Matthew, the language of witness and witnessing is confined to the legal sphere. Thus witnesses are no longer required in the trial of Jesus since he has condemned himself (Mark 14.63; Matt. 26.65), or the disciples will be dragged before governors and kings 'for a witness to them' (Mark 13.10; Matt. 10.18). This expression is usually taken to signify 'the opportunity to bear witness,' especially in Matthew's account where the phrase 'and to the Gentiles' is added, thus suggesting a wider horizon than the merely forensic.

In Luke's writings this shift to the more general usage becomes very obvious. At the end of the Gospel the Twelve are told: 'You are witnesses to these things' (Luke 24.48), with reference to the whole ministry of Jesus, which is to be understood as fulfilment of Moses and the prophets. Thus, their future mission of bearing witness to Jesus is already indicated, something that is confirmed at the beginning of Luke's second volume, Acts of the Apostles. There the disciples are commissioned to *witness* rather than to 'preach' (*kerysein*, Mark) or to 'teach' (*didaskein*, Matthew): 'You will be my witnesses in Jerusalem and Judaea and Samaria and to the end of the earth' (Acts 1.8). Subsequently, in the election of the replacement of Judas within the college of the Twelve, Luke spells out the conditions for appointment, namely, association with Jesus from the beginning and witness to his resurrection (Acts 1.21f.; see Acts 10.39; 13.31). Not merely does the term 'witness' apply to the Twelve, it can also be used for others like Paul, who within the narrative of Acts is the one to bring the witness to the Gentiles (Acts 22.15; 26.16), or Stephen, who is usually designated the first Christian martyr in the more restricted sense of shedding his blood for Christ, an event at which Paul, on his own admission, was present (Acts 22.20).

The Fourth Gospel also develops its own sense in which the language of witnessing is most appropriate for describing the mission of Jesus and the first Christians. The verb *martyreo*, 'to bear witness' occurs thirty-three times in the Gospel, in the vast majority of instances as a description for the activity of Jesus. His words and deeds are 'a bearing witness' to the fact that he has come from God and that his word is true. 'For this was I born and for this have I come into the world, to bear witness to the truth,' is the somewhat ironic proclamation of the Johannine Jesus as he is on trial before Pilate (John 18.37). This declaration of his life's purpose in a formal legal setting takes on a special resonance, since for the evangelist the whole ministry of Jesus represents the great trial of the world, as Jesus himself is made to declare earlier: 'For judgment (or, 'as an object of judgment') I have come into the world' (John 9.39). Jesus' coming constitutes the great crisis of the world in that people are summoned to opt now for the light rather than the darkness. A decision for light and truth rather than falsehood and darkness is called for now by recognizing Jesus as the light of the world – the way, the truth and the life (John 8.16; 12.31; 16. 8, 11).

This brief survey suggests the way in which a general term from the legal sphere gradually evolved into a technical term for the Christian missionary experience in a hostile world. Yet, paradoxically, with this evolution the term reverted to its original field of reference within the ambience of the law courts. It now described the Christian stance before Roman administrators, leading to the death sentence for refusal to worship the emperor and denounce Christ. It is only in the post-conciliar era that the Lukan and Johannine significance of the term as descriptive of the Christian mission in the world has been retrieved, so that it is possible again to speak meaningfully of a life of witness, open to all committed Christians, rather than the exceptional situation of the few who accept death by martyrdom without protest after the pattern of Jesus. In spite of this broader understanding of the notion of witness in the New Testament it is remarkable that Jesus himself is never called a *martys* – the use of the verb to describe his ministry in the Fourth Gospel is the closest one comes to such a conception. The absence is particularly striking in regard to the death of Jesus, since it provided the model for the subsequent martyrs, beginning with Stephen. We must explore this apparent lacuna further.

II. Interpreting the death of Jesus

'We proclaim Christ, a stumbling block to the Jews and foolishness to the Gentiles, but for those who are called, both Jew and Greek, Christ the power of God and the wisdom of God' (1 Cor. 1.23).

'I handed on to you as of first importance what I had received: that Christ died for our sins in accordance with the scriptures, that he was buried, and that he was raised on the third day in accordance with the scriptures' (1 Cor. 15.3–4).

'The Son of Man has come not to be served, but to serve and to give his life as a ransom for many' (Mark 10.46).

Without doubt the death of Jesus raised a serious question for his first followers. Paul addresses the issue directly: it was a stumbling block to the Jews who could only entertain as messiah someone who would introduce God's glorious reign, not die a criminal's death. For the Gentiles, on the other hand, especially the élites of Roman society in Corinth and elsewhere, the claim that such a shamed and shameful person could receive any honour from the gods or from humans was unthinkable, even derisory. Yet as the second and third citation above indicate, the early Christians had another resource, namely, the Hebrew scriptures, which enabled them to see the death of Jesus in a different light from that of uncommitted outsiders. Paul's formula 'he died for (on behalf of) our sins' and Mark's statement put on the lips of Jesus that he wants to be the servant whose life will be given as a ransom, or sin-offering for the many have clear echoes of the famous passage about the role of the suffering servant in Isaiah 53. This innocent figure's unjust humiliation and suffering is deemed redemptive for the many, and God eventually vindicates him.

The notion of a sacrifice for sin is derived from the priestly tradition dealing with the rites of the Day of Atonement (Lev. 16), and it offered one possibility for explaining the death of Jesus. In the Epistle to the Romans (3.21–26), Paul describes Jesus as the new 'mercy seat', that is, the place where the divine presence was deemed to dwell within the Holy of Holies, the cleansing of which was the central act of the atonement ritual. The high priest was allowed to enter the inner sanctuary where the mercy seat was located only once a year on *Yom Kippur* (the Day of Atonement). Even this most holy place was deemed to have been defiled by the sins of Israel and had to be purified through the sprinkling of the blood of the sacrificial victim. For Paul, however, it is the blood of Jesus that functions as the ultimate cleansing sacrifice of the sins of all humanity, Jews and Gentiles alike.

While Paul's development of the notion of the atoning death of Jesus is clearly inspired by the *Yom Kippur* rites, his description is somewhat dense with an overloading of images, as is often his wont. However, the author of the Epistle to the Hebrews turns the events of *Yom Kippur* into an elaborate contrastive allegory for explaining the efficacy of the sacrificial death of Jesus. In this presentation Jesus is both the high priest and the atoning victim. His death is seen as an entry into the heavenly holy place, 'which is not made with hands, that is, not of this creation'. In doing so he makes a once-for-all atonement for sin, unlike the high priest who enters the earthly sanctuary each year bearing the blood of another, not his own blood, and providing a rite of purification that offers only an external purification (Heb. 8–9).

This tradition of interpreting the death of Jesus in sacrificial terms drawn from the priestly strand of the Hebrew Bible was to have enormous influence in later Christian theological reflection. In the scholastic synthesis of mediaeval times, Jesus' atoning death and his divine status were the lynchpins of the system. Only a God-man could repair the damage done to the divine-human relationship by the original sin of our first parents, which each human inherits at birth. A sacrifice of infinite value was required in order to make satisfaction to an infinite God. In this perspective Jesus' death becomes divorced from his life, and his sole purpose is deemed to have lived so that he might die. This legalistic understanding of Jesus' death as satisfaction both distorted the understanding of God as a loving and caring Self

Jesus the Martyr 53

and undervalued completely the significance of Jesus' life. Since everything depended on the understanding of his death in sacrificial terms any other interpretation, including the idea of Jesus as martyr/witness, was precluded.

There were, however, other possibilities for understanding Jesus' death, which might have done greater justice to the historical significance of his life. One such figure, familiar within Jewish circles of the period, was the prophet or wise one, whose deaths were intimately related to their lives and the values which had informed them. Unlike the Greek tradition where the noble death was seen as bowing with equanimity and dignity to the inevitability of one's fate, the death of the prophet/wise one in the Jewish tradition was deemed noble because it was brought about through a passion for justice which fearlessly challenged the dominant ethos of the day. The prophet Jeremiah, who barely escaped with his life because he dared to challenge the Jerusalem aristocracy of his day, was the prototype of such a figure. In his case his oracles of doom and his personal life of being persecuted for his message are intimately interwoven, thus giving rise to a new type of literature, namely the Prophetic Life which in many ways was a forerunner to the Gospel genre in which Jesus' life and death were framed. There is a 'biographic' quality to the Suffering Servant of Isaiah 53 also, in which the implied author, a collective 'we', speaks. The manner in which the servant figure was treated shamefully and the reactions of others to him are described in gory detail without any realization of the value of that person, which only God could properly assess. In this instance, though there is recognition of the servant's life being treated as an atoning sacrifice for sin, as we have noted already, this does not exhaust all other aspects of the servant's biography.

The prophetic and wisdom traditions on the importance of such a life are fused in the first century BCE Alexandrian composition, the Book of Wisdom. The form is again that of a generalized narrative, not unlike the Isaiah passage, in which the fate of the wise one is narrated from the point of view of the opponents. They treated the wise shamefully because he reproached them for their sins against the law. These consisted in living sumptuous and arrogant lives, in the process ignoring the basic tenets of Jewish piety of caring for the poor and widows. Thus the very sight of the righteous wise one is a reproach to the evil ones 'because the manner of his life is unlike that of others and his ways are strange' (Wisd. 2.6–15). In the end there is a reversal of fortunes when the wicked realize their wickedness and the just are duly rewarded. The wealth of the wicked has vanished, but the righteous live forever: 'Their reward is with the Lord and the Most High takes care of them. Therefore they will receive a glorious crown, and a beautiful diadem from the hand of the Lord' (Wisd. 5.1–8, 15–16). There is no suggestion that the wise one(s) are actually put to death, yet the belief in after-life provides the author with the opportunity for describing the outcome of reversal of fortunes that eventually takes place.

Among the Gospel writers, Luke's account of Jesus fits this model of the persecuted prophet of justice most closely. It is interesting that in his version of the saying in Mark 10.46, cited at the outset of this section, Luke omits any mention of a life given 'as a ransom for many' (Luke 22.27). Instead Luke portrays Jesus as the champion of the poor and the challenger of the wealthy, who in the end is condemned on an explicitly political charge of 'perverting our nation' by 'forbidding the payment of taxes to Caesar', and he is accused of stirring up the people 'beginning from Galilee to this place' (Luke 23.2–5). As the self-proclaimed prophet of justice for all in accordance with the Jubilee tradition (Luke 4.18–20), Jesus refused to be intimidated by his opponents in Luke's account. Like other prophets before him, he must go to Jerusalem, even if that means death. Yet he ignores the warning to escape from a possible threat from Herod Antipas when advised by Pharisees about the danger (Luke 13.31–35). In terms of our discussion of the appropriateness of using the term *martys* for Jesus, it is surely significant that although, as we have seen, Luke has a preference for the term in relation to the early Christian mission, he does not apply it to Jesus himself, but reserves it for his followers. Is Luke conscious of the fact that Jesus represented the beginning of the movement, and as such it was for others to bear witness to him, while Jesus himself must be seen as the unique originator/prophet without whose life and death there never would have been a Christian movement? There is one final step to our investigation, therefore. Why did Jesus die, or in terms of a recent book about him *What killed Jesus?* Perhaps an attempted answer to this question may provide a better solution to the question of Jesus the Martyr.

III. Jesus' death: a challenge to the systems

Once we approach the question of Jesus' death from a historical rather than a theological perspective, we are thrown back into the world of Herodian Galilee and the need to understand the realities of Jesus' ministry within that context. However, unlike some recent treatments of the historical Jesus that focus almost exclusively on Galilee, treating the death in Jerusalem as virtually incidental, I believe that the whole thrust of Jesus' ministry had *both* Galilee *and* Jerusalem in its sights. Because of the popularity today of the 'Synoptic Jesus' who engages with the social structures of Galilee, we should not ignore the Johannine Jesus whose ministry is much more Jerusalem-oriented and engages with the Jerusalem temple and those who were the guardians of that system, namely, the Jerusalem priestly aristocracy. It is commonplace to accept that both the Synoptic and Johannine accounts are later theological reflections and the historian's task is to seek for the Jesus figure that has given rise to these accounts. When all due allowance is made for the different theological orientations of different groups of Jesus' followers and the complex process of memory and interpretation that has taken place, it should be recognized that behind both accounts is somebody who was active both in Galilee and Jerusalem. It could scarcely have been otherwise once it is accepted that Jesus is a Jewish prophet whose own self-understanding is grounded in various strands of Jewish restoration eschatology.

In Galilee Jesus encountered a Herodian administration that had made exorbitant demands on the local population in order to honour their Roman overlords. Herod Antipas, the son of Herod the Great, had been appointed ruler of the region by the emperor Augustus, but not with the title 'king', something he aspired to as the legitimate heir to his father. In order to win the favour of Rome he honoured the emperor by refurbishing his capital Sepphoris, giving him the title *autokrator*/sole ruler, and in 19 CE naming his new foundation by the lakeshore Tiberias, in honour of the new emperor. These two foundations, established while Jesus was a young adult in the village culture of Galilee, were a major disruption of that landscape. Together they symbolized the introduction of a whole new system of control and demand on the Jewish peasantry, contrasting sharply in terms of lifestyle, values and attitudes. The resources of the countryside – natural and human – were being deployed to support and sustain this affluent lifestyle with little being received back in return. The slide from landowner to leaseholder to day labourer was inexorable and inevitable. The values of a kinship society in sharing limited resources for the good of the group rather than individual needs were being rapidly eroded, giving rise to deep-seated tensions between the new Herodian élite and the established Jewish peasantry of the surrounding village culture.

'Those who are adorned in fine clothing are in the houses of kings,' was Jesus' pointed comment on this changing situation (Matt.11.17). Significantly, he is not said to have visited either Herodian foundation, but to have concentrated his ministry of healing and teaching to the lakeshore and the villages, even extending it beyond the confines of political Galilee – to the borders of Tyre, the villages of Caesarea Philippi and to the territory of the Gadarenes/Gerasenes. His teaching, often expressed in pithy, proverbial sayings and short stories of a parabolic nature, drew on the local imagery, but had a pointed message. Jesus espoused a value-system that was the direct antithesis of Rome's. The poor, not the powerful, were blessed; peace originated in the heart and was not imposed by the sword; wealth and affluence were no signs of God's favour. God's kingdom and not that of Rome would prevail. The kingdom and the house divided against itself could not survive, and already that was evident in the deposition of Archelaus in Judaea and the disputes between Antipas and his brother Philip, as to who had the right of succession. Jesus' healings were not the result of magic or done in association with the evil forces that were popularly deemed to control the lives of humans. Rather, they were signs of the in-breaking of God's kingdom now and with that the imminent demise of Rome and its clients, the Herodians.

In view of the challenge that Jesus' ministry posed to Roman rulers, both overtly and covertly, it is surprising that he did not suffer the same fate at the hands of Antipas as did his mentor John the Baptist. The Jewish historian, Josephus, gives a more reliable account of the latter's fate than do the Gospels. According to him John's popularity with the masses because of his espousal of justice for all alarmed Antipas, who feared a popular uprising that would undoubtedly have meant his own deposition by Rome. So John was apprehended, put in prison in Machaerus in Perea, and eventually murdered. It was in Jerusalem, not Galilee that Jesus came to the notice of Rome and its collaborators, the Jewish priestly aristocracy. His action in the temple – overturning the tables of the moneychangers and casting out the buyers and sellers – is the immediate cause of his arrest and eventual handing over to the Romans, according to the Synoptic accounts. However, it may be that that incident is made to carry too much weight in terms of the real cause of Jesus' death. Undoubtedly, the temple and its personnel as these had evolved in the Hellenistic and Roman periods were part of the exploitative system that was operative from the reign of Herod the Great at least.

The Fourth Gospel's account of Jesus' repeated challenge to the symbolism of the temple, claiming to be the sole means of access to God, with its pilgrimage, festivals and tithing, spells out the real implications of Jesus' kingdom-praxis, even in its Galilean setting. Once God's unconditional care and forgiveness can be experienced outside and independently of the officially designated channels – as Jesus both proclaimed and practised – then there was an inevitable clash between the charismatic and the institutional aspect of the Jewish religion. The fact that the form of Jesus' execution – crucifixion – was Roman rather than Jewish cannot obscure the fact that like other prophets before and after him, Jesus' life and message were unacceptable to the religious aristocracy. These were already discredited among the people at large because they had been imposed by Herod the Great at the expense of the Hasmonean predecessors and had colluded with direct Roman rule once this was imposed in Judea in the year 6 CE. As a country prophet Jesus must have known his eventual fate, but was undeterred in witnessing to his conviction that with his ministry God's kingdom had indeed begun to establish itself and that his own future would be taken care of, irrespective of how Rome's imperial power and Jerusalem's temple aristocracy might treat him.

Conclusion: Jesus, the faithful witness

Only once in the New Testament is the word *martys* applied to Jesus. Fittingly, this occurs at the beginning of the Book of Revelation (1.5), a document that celebrates the victory of 'Jesus, the faithful witness/martyr' (*pistos martys*). The author seeks to encourage those Christians of Asia Minor who in c. 90 CE suffered at the hands of the Roman emperor, Domitian. Those who have already paid the ultimate price for their loyalty have been able 'to wash their garments in the blood of the lamb' and so join in the triumphant heavenly celebration (7.14). Rome's demise is imminent, the readers are assured, to be replaced by the new Jerusalem that will descend from heaven, inaugurating the thousand-year reign of Christ and his elect. In the midst of a crisis it is important to be able to catch glimpses of the successful outcome.

In this highly imaginative work Jesus' fate at the hands of the Roman administration of Judaea is recalled and celebrated as a way of consoling and reassuring Christians, faced with the same opposition in another place and time, to be faithful also. By daringly recalling and celebrating his victory, Jesus the witness/martyr enables and emboldens others to follow in his footsteps. This was the pattern of Christian resistance that would continue up to the reign of Constantine, when at last the Christian church would no longer be persecuted but privileged by the power of Rome. Then, however, the demands were different if the 'faithful witness' of Jesus was to continue to inspire and encourage an alternative vision to that of imperial domination and exploitation. Christians were no longer asked to bear witness in the law-courts of the empire; their task now was to continue to challenge the imperial value systems as Jesus had done when he first encountered these in

Galilee. The fact that the memory of his challenge and resistance was still available in the gospel narratives ensured that some, at least, refused to accept the blandishments of empire, even when they came in a Christian dress. It is that memory that continues to inspire countless nameless ones to resist imperial structures in our world today, no matter how innocently these may appear. In doing so the *martys*/witness may easily become *martys*/martyr, without ever receiving the recognition of a formal trial. But that fate does not make their lives any less significant since their witnessing is done in the name of the one who did not cry out, but who fearlessly confronted the evil of human domination and exploitation, whether political or religious. Viewed from this perspective martyrdom comes in many guises. All that is required is to be faithful to the radical witness of Jesus.

Witnesses to Love, Killed by Hatred of Love

JOSÉ IGNACIO GONZÁLEZ FAUS

State of the question

Twenty years ago Karl Rahner wrote in this very journal, 'It is strange that the church should have canonized Maximilian Kolbe as a confessor and not as a martyr.'[1] Rahner was right to find it strange, but the fact was wrong, and very shortly afterwards he was awarded the status of a martyr. And yet when his canonization was decreed (1982), the members of the Roman Curia who had progressed the case declared him a 'confessor' as he had not died 'out of hatred of the faith'. If I am to believe the witness of a canon lawyer (whom I trust), the change was due to the insistence of Pope John Paul II, which left certain members of the Curia smarting and unhappy.

This anecdote is interesting not in itself but for what it demonstrates. It is a fact that shortly after the martyrdom of Archbishop Romero, official voices declared that he could not be called a martyr as he had not died *in odium fidei*. To which Rahner once again replied that Maria Goretti had not exactly been killed out of hatred of the faith, and yet the church had proclaimed her a martyr.[2]

Both stories oblige us to try to define this 'hatred of the faith' a little more clearly, especially as Jesus was not killed out of hatred of the faith but *in the name of a faith* (or, in any case, out of hatred for the consequences that Jesus drew from his experiences of God). And it would not seem possible for Christians to remain untroubled if it is argued that their 'witnesses' (which is what 'martyrs' means) bear no relation to the One who is called 'the faithful witness'.[3]

I. Who is a martyr?

1. Shift in the concept of martyrdom

As far as I am aware, the notion of 'hatred of the faith' does not appear in early theological tradition. It stems from Pope Benedict XIV's 1737 treatise on canonizations, which was undoubtedly valuable as it helped to instil order and to eliminate a lot of mythology. But now it seems outdated.

When it was first used, the stress in the phrase *in odium fidei* probably fell more on 'hatred' than on 'faith'. Those killed out of hatred are compared to those who are killed not passively but in their struggle for the faith or 'defending the republic from attack by enemies who propose the destruction of the faith', as St Thomas puts it. Aquinas also asked if these soldiers could not equally be considered martyrs. And even though his suggestion was not officially accepted, the reason he gives in support of it is important: *they placed the common good above their individual good*.[4]

But at the height of the Counter-Reformation, and on account of the polemic against the Protestant notion of faith as trust, which led to an exaggerated intellectualizing of the Catholic notion of faith, *the accent began to shift from the word 'hatred' to the word 'faith'*. And faith was also understood in a purely noetic manner and in contradistinction to praxis and the life of the believer. So martyrs came to be viewed as those who die only for a doctrine or an intellectual system. And here we have the current understanding of *in odium fidei*, which explains the two anecdotes at the start of this article.

By the time we reach the twentieth century, this view has disastrous consequences, since according to this understanding, it seems that *only an unbeliever can bring about martyrs*. A Christian, however cruel he may be, cannot produce them because, if he calls himself a Christian, he will not hate the faith. Hence the perplexity produced by so many Latin American martyrs who gave up their lives out of love – just as Jesus did – at the hands of officials who called themselves Christian and who could move from torturing to helping to distribute communion in their parish churches, or to playing tennis with the papal nuncio.[5] The perplexity and this contrast were very well expressed by Juan Hernández Pico: 'Martyrdom in Latin America today scandalizes the authorities and sectors of the church still allied to them, because the martyrs come from a church that has emigrated from its home among the powerful to the impoverished masses.'[6]

We can without irony say that the reason for the scandal is that the notion of revelation had also 'emigrated' earlier, from being a manifestation of God's love to being one of abstract truths, removed from people's lives and of which the ecclesiastical authorities were the depository and the guardians. All this makes it essential that we now re-focus this unfocussed idea of martyrdom. And to do this we need to delve for a moment into theological tradition.

2. Theological tradition

In effect: before the anti-Protestant polemic over faith, St Thomas had asked whether the cause of martyrdom 'is only faith'.[7] He begins his answer, 'It seems that it is', which indicates that the true answer is that it is not. Here are some of the reasons Thomas adduces for this:

1. Martyrs do not bear witness to any truth but to a truth that is *secundum pietatem*. This is a difficult phrase to translate, but I hope I am not doing it a disservice if I render it for today as a 'praxic' truth, since it is just at this point that Aquinas brings in the example of John the Baptist (see note 2).

2. In his answer to the third objection, he comments that, precisely because 'the cause of martyrdom is a *divine* good', it follows that 'any human being can embrace the cause of martyrdom if it is *referred to God*'. Martyrdom is a divine good because it is a gift of God, not because it concerns a divine truth considered in the abstract.

3. Precisely because of this, St Thomas defines the martyr as a 'witness to the perfection of love'.[8] And he is furthermore convinced that *justice* is a component of this perfection of love.

4. Indeed, in the preceding article he states that, in martyrdom, a person 'does not abandon faith *and justice* even when faced with imminent death'. And elsewhere he stresses that those who 'suffer for Christ are not only those who suffer for the faith of Christ but also those who suffer for *any work of justice* out of love of Christ'.[9] The expression '*any* work' restrains any attempt to reduce justice to a mere interior disposition. And in a world like ours, in which the central sin is the socio-historical oppression of thousands of millions of children of God, these clarifications by St Thomas are absolutely indispensable.

St Thomas' teaching on this was taken up by the Second Vatican Council: 'By martyrdom a disciple is transformed into an image of his Master, who freely accepted death on behalf of the world's salvation; he perfects that image even to the shedding of blood . . . The Church, therefore, considers martyrdom as an exceptional gift and as the highest proof of love' (LG 42, 4, 3). The church may do so: the Roman Curia, it seems, does not, as indicated by the two anecdotes at the start of this article. The Vatican II text does not waste words, and it is worth emphasizing three points in it:

1. *Martyrdom in the church has to be assimilated to the martyrdom of Jesus.* A notion of martyrdom that cannot be applied to the Master makes no sense. Martyrdom is an assimilation to 'the death of Christ', who, as I have remarked above, did not die exactly from *odium fidei*.

2. Precisely because of this, martyrdom is a gift: '*an exceptional gift*', the Council calls it.

3. *Martyrdom is, above all, a proof of love*. Martyrs can be called *testes charitatis*. And here John Paul II was quite right, as against those Curia members who worried about calling Maximilian Kolbe a martyr.

The importance of these three points becomes clearer if they are set a little deeper in context. The Vatican II definition cited comes in a section headed with a quotation from I John 4.16: 'God is love, and he who abides in love abides in God, and God in him.' And the paragraph from which the second sentence of our quotation comes begins, 'Since Jesus, the Son of God, *manifested his charity by laying down his life for us*' (my italics). In my view, excluding all these features from our concept of martyrdom would be downright heterodox and would reflect only terror of the implications of the words by Hernández Pico already cited.[10]

But it is not even necessary to advance as far as Vatican II. I could have stuck with Trent, which taught that faith does not deserve the name of faith 'if it is not informed by love', because it would then be 'a dead and useless faith' (DS 1571). It would then seem that those who opposed calling Maximilian Kolbe and Oscar Romero martyrs should define martyrdom as violent death inflicted *in odium fidei mortuae et otiosae*. Let them look to it.

In this way, definition of martyrdom is focussed more on the *motives of those who die and not exclusively on the motives of those who kill*. By paying more attention to the victim than to the executioner, we recover the terminology of the early church, for which a martyr was primarily a 'witness'. Witness to the truth of the God who is love, in a world ruled by hatred and selfishness. Witness to that truth with the testimony of his or her life, not merely with abstract teaching. And exceptional witness because the gift of one's life is the supreme expression of love. The New Testament had already made it clear that Christian existence is conflictive (cf. 1 Thess. 3.3–4), and it can be no different in a world order built on money in place of love and on the pretensions to power of its various 'emperors'.[11]

At the time of Jesus and the first Christians, the divinization of the emperor was a factor carrying greater social weight than the divinization of money typical of our world. I shall comment on this difference below, but in the meantime it is worth drawing the consequences, very briefly, of what I have just argued. According to this, apart from being a gift *of God*, they are a *conflictive* gift, as they cannot fail to be in a world structured on sin. Hence the tendency of certain church authorities to forget about them.

These church authorities remind me of the philosopher Celsus, who objected to Christians, on the grounds that 'if everyone did as you do, the emperor would be left alone and abandoned, and dominion of the world would be passed to the barbarians outside the law'.[12] It seems to me difficult to deny that these words could almost have come from the famous Santa Fe Document, which warned the emperor Reagan against the Catholic Church and liberation theology as dangerous to the interests of the empire.

II. Two discourses

1. From victims to witnesses

In the early church there seem to have been two discourses relating to martyrdom. The first, closer to the Stoic mentality of fortitude or the Socratic teaching on wisdom, is found in certain allusions by Ignatius of Antioch or Justin.[13] But at the same time as this discourse is current, the intuition of Revelation is soon recovered: Jesus is the supreme *victim* who has become the 'faithful *witness*' for us.

In accordance with this, the Shepherd of Hermas places the *martys* (witness) in continuity with the *homologetes* (confessor). This continuity can be seen when just a little later the Apostolic Tradition of Hippolytus considers that the mere fact of being a confessor can equate to ordination to ministry in the church: the readiness to give one's life (which characterized the confessors, even if they were not called on to do so) is a sort of supreme teaching office, capable of engendering faith. This why the *Martirium Polycarpi* tells us that he was 'not merely an illustrious *teacher*, but also a conspicuous *martyr*'.[14]

Giving one's life is, then, for a Christian, the supreme teaching. And this element of surrender ought to be present throughout the teaching office of believers. But for personal surrender to reach the point of giving one's life is a gift that no one can claim for him- or herself and that is seen as a special way of conforming to Christ. And so it is that the martyr Polycarp is described as a sharer in Christ (*Christoû koinônos*; VI). The martyr is a teacher through the intensity of his teaching: he has put 'the love of God in Christ Jesus our Lord' (Rom. 8.39) and the one lordship of Jesus (I Cor. 8.6) into effect.

It is not hard to see that this conception accords much better with that of Vatican II and with St Thomas than with that of the Counter Reformation, the sombre consequences of which I have already alluded to. We now need to draw the consequences that result from this prior concept of martyrdom.

2. From witnesses to victims

The first conclusion is very basic: *if there are martyrs it is because there are victims*. Reclaiming the phrase 'hatred of love' allows us to state this, and so to incorporate the victims of Latin America into the subject of martyrdom. There are an impressive number of these: anonymous 'disappeareds'; indigenous people of Brazil and Guatemala; many of the mothers and grandmothers of the Plaza de Mayo, still trying to establish the paternity of a son or granddaughter. Many of them are not merely victims but true anonymous martyrs, like those the martyrology of my own country calls 'the innumerable martyrs of Zaragoza'.

I should also like to reclaim the term 'victims', since speaking of them necessarily involves speaking of *executioners*. And the fact that the executioners in such a holocaust have not been pagan emperors, or atheist states, or non-Christian Nazi regimes, but people who professed the faith and did not hate it, presents the church with an unavoidable and very simple question: *What has happened?*

We need to ask – in a negative tone – what has happened for the official church not to have known how to be sensitive to this. What has happened to make the bishops of Argentina say not a word on the martyrdom of Enrique Angelelli until twenty-five years had elapsed – and then only a pretty vague word. What has happened – answering positively – to make Christianity in Latin America to recover through its martyrs its primary identity as affirmed by Romero and Ellacuría. Because the posibility of laying down one's life belongs to the core of the Christian faith. And finally what has happened in the most generic sense of that view of the world that some years ago led Pedro Casaldáliga to write these words (which I have quoted before) on the victims, in a work dedicated to martyrdom:

> For some time – since, in fact, I came into everyday contact with the indigenous populations – I have felt the disappearance of whole peoples as an absurd mystery of historical iniquity, which reduces me to the most abject sort of faith: 'Lord, why have you abandoned them?' How can the Bread of Life, the creative Spirit of every culture, allow these multiple annihilations?[15]

No form of piety, no reclamation of the religious and sacred dimension can make the two dimensions this text brings to light disappear: *the mystery of wickedness* (in Europe it seems that evil and sin no longer exist, unless I believe someone is doing them to me), and *Jesus' question: Why have you abandoned me?* Any form of piety that does not hold these two points to be central will have deserted the cross of Christ and will not deserve the appellation of 'Christian', not even on the supposition that it is once again giving Rome a splendour that the Vatican feels it has lost and is trying to recover.

I understand that taking reclamation of both themes seriously will exhaust us and make us lose sleep, and also that we lack the strength to do it in such a hedonistic society as that of the developed world. I certainly do. But I have to say that this discomfort should be our (and the Roman Church's) small dose of martyrdom, for those of us who are not called to the divine wonder of the martyrs. We bear it out of solidarity with them – and also to make us into 'slightly credible' witnesses.

Conclusion

Martyrdom can be defined as a fullness of meaning that springs precisely from renouncing what seems to be 'the basic meaning': life. A fullness of meaning that is absolutely beyond our powers. Martyrdom is a gift of God to the martyr, and martyrs are a gift of God to the people of God. Because they are witnesses to faith through being witnesses to the 'greater love'.

Precisely because of this, to forget the martyrs is not merely carelessness or a device for keeping our own psychological health. To forget the martyrs is simply to turn a deaf ear to a teaching, to close our eyes or harden our hearts so that they cannot get to us. The words of the psalmist, 'Oh that today you would listen to his voice: harden not your hearts!' can be applied paradigmatically to those who forget the martyrs.

Translated by Paul Burns

Notes

1. K. Rahner, 'Dimensions of martyrdom: a plea for the broadening of a classical concept' in J.-B. Metz and E. Schillebeeckx (eds), 'Martyrdom Today', *Concilium* 163, March 1983, pp. 9–11.
2. As in so many cases, Rahner was being more authentically traditional than his opponents. St Thomas also regarded those who died in defence of virginity as martyrs. And elsewhere he argues that the church celebrates the martyrdom of John the Baptist, who was not killed out of hatred for the faith but because he condemned an adultery (2a 2ae, 124, 5, c).
3. *ho martys ho pistos*, Rev. 1.5.
4. Cf. *In IV Sent*. Dis. 49, q5, a3, *quaestiunculae* 2 and 3.

5. Not to mention the Spanish civil war, in which it has always been supposed that only those who died *on one side* could be beatified. Not those who died on the other, even if they were Christians or priests who died for their way of viewing the faith. And they existed.
6. 'Martyrdom today in Latin America: stumbling-block, folly and power of God' in *Concilium* 163 (n.1), pp. 37–42.
7. *Summa theologica*, II, II, q. 124, art. 5.
8. '*maxime demonstrat perfectionem charitatis*'.
9. Commentary *ad romanos*, ch. 8, lect. 7.
10. Before the council, Sebastian Tromp, in his *De revelatione divina*, defined martyrdom as 'the voluntary acceptance of death inflicted *ex odio fidei vel legis divinae*' (348). I have ended the quotation in Latin to show that faith is identified with the divine law (the text has *vel*, not *aut*), which is one way of alluding to human praxis, as opposed to a merely intellectual concept of faith.
11. It is worth noting that often when Jesus appears conflictive in the Gospels, it is said shortly before that 'he was moved to compassion'.
12. Origen, *Contra Celsus* VIII, 68 in PG 11, 1619; see also VIII, 73 (PG 11, 1627) on divinization of the emperors and military service.
13. 'They can kill me but they cannot harm me', Socrates quoted in *Apologia* I, 24.
14. Para. XIX, 1. See J. Stevenson (ed), revd by W. H. C. Frend, *A New Eusebius*, London 1987, p. 28 [trans.].
15. P. Casaldáliga, 'The "Crucified" Indians – a case of anonymous collective martyrdom' in Concilium 163 (n.1), p. 51.

The Servant of Yahweh: The Patient Endurance of the Poor, Mirror of God's Justice

CARLOS MESTERS

Ceará, Brazil, 1979. We were at a four-day biblical reunion for agricultural workers. At the end of the third day they organized a round-table discussion on the subject of the problem of the suffering of the poor. One of them, Don Raimundo, said, 'I am willing to take up the cross, but only the one that leads to the liberation of the people.' Dona Dalva replied, 'Don Raimundo, I agree. But what is the cross that brings the people liberation? At home I've got a child. He's got paralysis. Now it's made him an idiot. He can't walk or talk. There's only me to take care of him, the whole time. What do I do with this suffering? Does it bring liberation to the people? And does it do anything for my child?' Raimundo had no answer to this.

Dalva's suffering demolished Raimundo's well-arranged ideas. The suffering of the people questions established ideas. There is a poem that says, 'Faced with the life of the patient people / we cannot speak; we can only be silent. / We forget our ideas of the wisdom of the people / and learn to be humble and begin to think.' Dalva's question provides a key for understanding the songs of the Servant of Yahweh. For their part, the songs throw light on the sufferings of the people.

I. A little background

The songs of the servant of Yahweh are found in the book of Isaiah (42.1–9; 49.1–6; 50.4–9; 52.13–53.12). Their origin goes back to a group of male and female disciples of Isaiah living during the Babylonian captivity some 550 years before Christ. Today many people ask who this Servant is supposed to be: is he the people, one of the prophets, Jesus, ourselves? The songs themselves do not make clear who he represents; they do not say. So whom could the writer have had in mind when he (or she) included the songs in the book?

One possible answer is this: the inspiration for the image of the Servant came from the person of the prophet Jeremiah, the epitome of suffering, who struggled for twenty-three years against the oppressors of the people without the slightest success (Jer. 25.3). Even then, he did not stop or abandon hope. He went on struggling for a further twenty years, until his death, still without success. The suffering people identified with him and saw a picture of their own lives in him.

The songs were included in the book of Isaiah not to tell the story of Jeremiah's life but to provide the exiled people with a model that would help them discover their mission to be People of God in the figure of the Servant. In fact, the context makes clear that the Servant of Yahweh is the suffering people. Chapters 40 to 55 are like the frame surrounding a picture. The picture (the songs) does not say who the Servant is, but the frame (the context) shows that *the Servant is the people*. We need only check the following texts: Isaiah 41.8–9; 42.18–20; 43.10; 44.1–2; 44.21; 45.4; 48.20; 54.17. All these, in one way or another, speak of the Servant as being the people. Those who forget to look at the title displayed on the frame run the risk of not understanding the picture.

The Servant is the people. But which people? He is the people in captivity, described in the fourth song as an oppressed, suffering, disfigured people, no longer appearing human and living in sub-human conditions; an exploited, mistreated and silenced people, without grace or beauty, full of suffering, avoided by others like lepers, condemned as criminals, defenceless and deprived of justice (53.2–8). A perfect picture of a third of the human race today!

In the songs of the Servant, God shows his preference for the poor and entrusts them with an important mission for the future of humankind, a mission that they alone, the oppressed, are in a position to carry out. The four songs are a sort of primer to help the oppressed, then and now, to discover and take on this mission of theirs.

The first song (Isa. 42.1–9) describes how God chooses the oppressed people to be his Servant. The second (49.1–6) shows how this people, still without faith in itself, discovers its mission. The third (50.4–9) tells how the people take up their mission and carry it out despite persecutions. The fourth (52.13–53.12) is a prophecy dealing with the future of the Servant and of his mission. A summary of the four songs (61.1–2) defines the people's mission.

II. The first three songs: the first three steps

1. First song: Isaiah 42.1–9

God addresses the human race and presents it with his favourite Servant, saying, 'He will not cry out or lift up his voice, or make it heard in the street; a bruised reed he will not break, and a dimly burning wick he will not quench' (42.2). Here the Servant is the one who, when persecuted, will not persecute; when oppressed, will not oppress; when bruised, will not bruise. In him the virus of violence and of the ruling ideology meets a barrier, which it cannot penetrate. This attitude of the Servant is the root of justice, which, by God's command, is to be implanted in the world.

God then addresses the Servant, telling him that he has called him 'in righteousness' (42.6). God desires to be just! Justice, which God wants to see implanted in the world, is hidden in the stubborn dignity of those poor people who do not break the bruised reed or quench the burning wick. For this reason, out of duty to justice, God calls him to be his servant and gives him the mission to spread this justice throughout the whole world.

The people of the poor, however, have trouble believing in the call, since the evidence of reality is the opposite. God calls them to establish 'justice in the earth' (42.4), but their situation makes them say, 'my right is disregarded by my God' (40.27). God calls them 'in righteousness' (42.6), but the people feel aggrieved at God himself and cry out, 'Judge my cause' (Lam. 3.59). God calls for the people to be united (42.6), but events make them protest, 'You have made us like sheep for slaughter, and have scattered us among the nations' (Ps. 44.12). God chooses them to be a 'light to the nations' (Isa. 42.6), but the people sigh, 'He has made me sit in darkness' (Lam. 3.6). God calls them to open the eyes of the blind (Isa. 42.7), but the people have no light for their own eyes: 'Who is blind but my servant?' (42.19). God calls them to 'bring out prisoners from the dungeon' (42.7), but the people groan that they are 'hard driven . . . [and] given no rest' (Lam. 5.5).

Crushed by pain, they have to proclaim the end of suffering; with their rights trampled, they must establish justice on the earth; despised by other peoples, they have to be a light to the nations; blind, they must shed light; captives, they must set free; practically dead, they have to give life; living in the darkness, they have to be a beacon! God's call appears to be a 'stumbling block [and] foolishness' (I Cor. 1.23) and still does so today. It took a long time for the people to begin to believe in this call. The course of this gradual discovery is described in the second song.

2. Second song: Isaiah 49.1–6

In this song, the Servant describes how he discovered the mission and so revolutionized his life. Just like so many of the poor today, he thought his life had no value or meaning and that his resistance to the virus of the system was in vain. He had said, 'I have laboured in vain, I have spent my strength for nothing and vanity' (49.4). Today they say, 'The little I can do counts for nothing. The system is stronger!' But for Isaiah's disciples it was just this patient endurance of the exiled people that made them the Servant of God. The very situation that produced their discouragement began to be a reason for understanding and hope. The people who were living without any consciousness of their worth began to discern the other side of reality, God's side, and discovered their mission: 'I will give you as a light to the nations, that my salvation may reach to the end of the earth' (49.6).

Where did this surprising consciousness of their mission, a consciousness that far surpassed all the premises present in the exiled people, come from? The people seemed to be a new creation!

What claims our attention in the whole of the second part of the book of Isaiah is the personal and virtually physical dimension of the images used to express this new experience of God and of life. God is experienced as *father* and *mother* (46.3; 49.15; 63.16), as *husband* and *bridegroom* of the people (54.5; 62.5). The exiled people are compared to a little child nourished by milk from God's 'consoling breast' and 'dandled on her knees' (66.11–13). The daughter of Zion, the bride, once forsaken and desolate, will again feel cherished and loved (62.4). God is marrying his people (62.5), gathering his children back under his protection (54.4–8), offering them help and comfort in a way never seen before (41.8–14; 49.13–16).

Such images reveal the conditions in which the exiles were condemned to live. They were living uprooted and lost in a captivity imposed by the Persian empire. All they had left, as with so many refugees today, was their family, people close to them: father, mother, husband, wife, children . . . and their bodies, the little world of house and neighbourhood, and some religious traditions. Nothing else! It was in the ambit of this family nucleus, so fragile and so insignificant compared to the omnipresent might of the empire, that they supported themselves in their resistance to the virus of the system. It was from this 'grain of mustard' that everything was rebuilt! It was from there that the new experience of God stemmed and the new understanding of their mission sprang. All this generated a new way of living, which is described in the third song.

3. Third song: Isaiah 50.4–9

Here, from the start, the Servant presents himself as a disciple, and he describes how he carries out his mission. Every day, in the morning, he tries to listen to what God has to tell him, so that he can 'sustain the weary with a word' (50.4). A disciple does not absolutize his own ideas but is open to learning. The clear understanding of God's support strengthens him. He no longer turns his face away from those who spit on him or tear out his beard. His face is 'set like flint'; he stands firm! The knowledge that God is helping him enables him to overcome his fear (50.7–8). Even if he is defeated, he fights in the certainty of eventual victory, knowing that God is helping and vindicating him (50.8–9).

This testimony by the Servant shows that there has been a great advance from the first to the third songs. The humble people, though still without understanding, who though bruised did not bruise in return, who though oppressed did not oppress, have gradually discovered their own dignity and mission. They now know that their cross is the seed of the new justice that God seeks to establish in the world: it is the road to liberation. The unjust and oppressive system is destined to fall to pieces (50.9).

But here, at the end of the third song, Dalva and Raimundo's question reappears, almost unnoticed. The discovery of the mission, described in the second song, and the very conscious resistance described in the third, could give the impression that those capable of carrying out the Servant's mission are only the few, like Raimundo, who are capable of discerning the situation and actively confronting the unjust system. The rest, those like Dalva and the bulk of the poor who simply suffer and endure – the old, the sick, the mad, the blind, AIDS sufferers, migrants, the disabled, those in hospitals and hospices, those who live under bridges and arches in the big cities, the excluded, the millions of exiles and the starving – will not share in the Servant's mission, since most of them know nothing about the system that oppresses them or are in any position to take an active part in the struggle for justice. The servant would then be not the whole of the oppressed people but just a more conscious group who march in front carrying the banner of liberation.

Dalva does not agree with this. She wants to take part in the struggle, and she wants a place for her brain-damaged and paralysed child. Like her, many people would like to know: 'Does the struggle of the cancer patient, dying alone in a bed, abandoned by all, have a liberating value for the whole of the people or not?' Still others ask, 'What does enduring like this achieve? Does it have a future? Consciousness and the struggle for justice will grow, that's true. But repression and suffering will grow to the same extent. What is the future of this Servant's struggle against the system? Is it worth holding out and struggling?' This is the problem that is tackled in the fourth song.

III. The fourth song: the future of the Servant and his mission

In effect, faced with the sometimes irritating slowness of the poor and the brutality of organized injustice, the Servant falls into the temptation of thinking that he alone is in a position to liberate the oppressed. He will be the leader and the judge of the liberation movement, since he alone knows the route. In this case, he would cease to be the *Servant* and would become the *Master*.

This temptation appears in a thousand guises in any liberation movement. It may be the reason why the great revolutions of history, even if they have done good things, have not succeeded completely in achieving the liberation of the oppressed, in the name of which all of them started. They failed to attend the school of the poor and learn the wisdom of the age-long endurance of the poor, a wisdom that is much older than the latest theories and also more lasting. Haste to show results does not allow them to make the marriage between new theory and ancient practice.

This was also the temptation that Jesus faced several times: when the devil encouraged him to turn stones into bread (Matt. 4.1–4); when the people wanted to make him a king (John 6.15); when Peter rebuked him for talking of his death (Mark 8.32–33). But taking his guidance from what he had learned from his Father and from the poor, and keeping the two together, Jesus made the fourth song his criterion for rejecting this temptation as the work of Satan (Mark 8.33). Jesus had come not to be a master but to be the Servant of all and to give his life in this service (Matt. 20.28). He made the summary of the four songs in Isaiah 61.1–2 the basis of his mission (Luke 4.16–21).

Fourth song: Isaiah 52.13 to 53.12

The fourth song describes the final battle between God's justice and the injustice of society. The victory will go to the Servant, 'beyond human semblance, and his form beyond that of mortals' (52.14). He 'shall prosper; he shall be exalted and lifted up, and shall be very high' (52.13). The defeated one shall conquer! 'That which had not been told them they shall see'

(52.15). How are we to understand such a form of victory? Reason alone, or ideas such as Raimundo's alone, cannot grasp its meaning.

It will be the victory not of the strong man who *conquers* his adversary through the power of his might, but of the oppressed who *convinces* his oppressor through the power of his witness. The fourth song is the public and collective confession of the oppressors, who, converted by the witness of the Servant, recognize their faults (53.6), admit that they have caused the Servant's suffering (53.4), and accept that they themselves have been saved and liberated by the Servant (53.5).

Following the introduction, in which God proclaims the Servant's victory (52.13–15), the converted oppressors begin their evidence by asking, 'Who has believed what we have heard? And to whom has the arm of the Lord been revealed?' (53.1). And directly after this they make a public confession in which they describe, by five interlinked degrees, the process of their conversion, brought about by the persistence of the Servant's fidelity to belief that it is possible, through love, to convince people to set their enemies free.

First degree: before the conversion (53.2–4). They thought the sufferings of the poor were a punishment from God. The poor would be guilty of their own misery. Today they say that poverty is the result of prejudice.

Second degree: beginnings of conversion (53.4–6). They begin to understand that the poor, in reality, are impoverished. They, the oppressors, have impoverished them. And now, finally, they recognize this: the Servant 'was wounded for our transgressions, crushed for our iniquities'.

Third degree: deepening of conversion (53.7–9). They acknowledge the patience and endurance of the Servant, of the poor. Bruised, the poor do not bruise in return; condemned by hunger and injustice, they are not corrupted, nor do they adopt the oppressors' methods to avenge themselves.

Fourth degree: conversion expressed in prayer (53.10). In a sincere prayer addressed to God, the oppressors recognize their liberator in the people they have oppressed and ask God to confirm the people in this mission. (The most likely translation of this verse would run: 'Oh, Lord! May your Servant, broken by suffering, be pleasing to you! / Accept his life as a sacrifice of expiation! / May he be able to see his descendants, have a long life, / and may your plan be realized through him!')

Fifth degree: God accepts their prayer (53.11–12). God responds to the plea of the converted oppressors, affirming that the way marked out by the Servant is the road leading to the justice that he, God, desires for all.

The Servant does not *conquer* through force but *convinces* through his enduring and patient witness to God's justice and to his love 'to the end'

(John 13.1). The victory then comes about simply by God giving a person strength to endure and hold out to the end!

IV. Questions left for today

When will the financiers, the directors of multinationals, the rulers of the world, the industrialists, the absentee landowners, the aristocrats, look at the world's poor, whom they are exploiting, and say, 'Truly, you are just, and we are the guilty'? When will the wealthy nations come to accept that the world's future cannot come from them but from the poor nations they dominate? When will the European Union take stock of the liberating project hidden under the patient and lengthy resistance of the anonymous peoples of the countries colonized by them for centuries in Africa, Asia, and Latin America? When will Raimundo give Dalva's handicapped son a place of honour in his community? When will the groups struggling for liberation stop trusting only in their own ideas about the people and begin also to believe in the people so as to accept new ideas from them?

When will the leaders of the church recognize that the church, rather than being *Mater et magistra*, should be, like Jesus, 'child and disciple' of the Father and of the poor?

When will the oppressed have the courage to say, 'Father, forgive them, for they know not what they do'?

When will all of us learn to recognize and to expel the oppressor who lives within us and who threatens us at every moment with the virus of the ruling ideology?

When, finally, shall we love our enemies?

Translated by Paul Burns

Martyrdom in Religious Traditions

FELIX WILFRED

As the elephant in the battlefield withstands the arrows shot from a bow, even so will I endure abuse; verily most people are lacking in virtue.
                                                    Buddhism, *Dhammapada* 320

Martyrdom, in a sense, is a social construct. For martyrs are the creation of a religious community which endues the suffering and death of an individual with meaning bearing upon its own identity, history, belief-system, rituals, etc. Precisely for this reason, martyrdom turns out to be something ambiguous in nature. As such, one group's martyrs can easily be terrorists for another group; one religious community's heroes could be the militant fundamentalists of another group. Bhindranwale is a revered martyr for the Sikh community; but he was at one time the most wanted terrorist of India. The ambiguous character connected with religious martyrdom lends itself to political extrapolation. A nation or ethnic group has its martyr-heroes symbolizing its national or ethnic consciousness, cementing the group's common identity and enhancing its power. The narratives of the passion of a community's martyrs, understandably, take on mythical forms and serve social and political purposes.

I. The power of death and the control of its meaning

Martyrdom is a voluntary laying down of one's life for the sake of some ultimate values such as truth, love, justice and freedom. In the last analysis, religions and religious communities possess the great power to interpret death in ultimate terms. In most cases, religions have viewed the natural process of ageing and dissolution as a poor mode of death, while they have extolled violent death faced with courage. In the Christian tradition, for example, the day of a martyr's death has been viewed as the day of his or her real birth (*dies natalis*).

The ideal of martyrdom is not entirely the creation of religious traditions.

Religions have often re-worked on the cultural heritage of various peoples. For example, the martyrdom of early Christians in Rome cannot be separated from the Roman cultural heritage of valour and glorious death in battle. The same could be said also of the Germanic peoples in whose culture the brave death of heroes has been exalted. For religions, what is involved in martyrdom is something more than the fearlessness in death honoured by the classical tradition. The honour of intrepid death is turned into something *sacred* by religions. For what is most feared – death – itself gets conquered by the heroic death of the martyrs. The fusion of the classical cultural approach and the Christian faith approach could be observed in the case of military martyrs in early Christianity.[1]

There seems to be a tradition in most religions according to which, not only death undergone for the sake of one's faith, but any violent ending of life, is considered as martyrdom. In Islam, the expression *shahid* or witness or martyr is used beyond the religious context to signify people who die in childbirth, through plague, drowning or any kind of sudden death as in an accident. In popular Hinduism, those who are killed unjustly for such reasons as transgressing the traditional caste-code are considered to be so powerful that they are turned into gods and goddesses. It need not be always in the case of physical death. There is a religious tradition, particularly in Hinduism, according to which anyone who sacrifices himself or herself for the cause of justice is someone with power. This goes with the Indian classical conviction – shared also by Buddhism and Jainism – that the self-emptying or nothingness is power-laden. On the contrary, it is the situation of possession which is one of weakness. This is something which we can attest in everyday life. People who have nothing to lose are the most free and daring. This potential can, of course, be exploited. Suicide bombers are often recruited from those who have lost their all – their possessions, kith and kin – and been subjected to great humiliations by the aggressors.

In the creation of martyrs there is a conflict to control the meaning of death. The community to which the martyr belongs is also the claimant for interpreting his or her death. It rejects outright any distortion of the meaning of this death by the slayers and persecutors. The fear that the power of death may be exploited by the community of the victim has haunted the persecutors. As a result, in not a few cases, the persecutors have chosen to eliminate any remnants of the victim, so that it does not become a rallying point for the aggrieved community. That is why persecutors have preferred to burn the bodies of the victims and scatter their ashes or to bury them clandestinely in mass graves.

In this regard we need to add a word on the way religious traditions prepare the 'martyrs' to appropriate suffering.[2] Religions differ from one another by their approach to human fallibility and the way they try to account for human suffering. These different explanations also characterize their approach to life, truth and human emancipation. Martyrdom implies profession of an ideology, and in the case of religions, it is the ensemble of religious beliefs, rituals and ethical injunctions. In this light, religions have created theological explanations and motifs to appropriate suffering and violent death. For Christians, it is the cross of Christ which seasons and prepares the disciples to appropriate suffering, whereas for other religious traditions it could be the law of *karma* as in Hinduism, or any other similar motif. In general, a continuous spiritual pedagogy on sacrifice and renunciation prepares the religious believers to the appropriation of suffering and even of heroic death.

II. Martyrdom in the light of religion and violence

1. Justification of violence

Religious traditions value the violent ending of life. They glorify and venerate the heroes who laid down their lives. This has deeper roots in what appears to be a persistent tradition connecting religion and violence. For Freud the religious enactment of violence, as is the case for example in ritual, is the way to a peaceful society. The sacrificial rituals and similar ones are channels to let go the human aggressiveness. For René Girard, it is the 'mimetic desire' which goes to explain an intrinsic connection between religion and violence. Ritually violence is transposed to the 'scapegoat' and performed as sacrifice, to become religiously sanctioned violence.[3] This nexus is seen also in terms of justification for violence. There are, in modern times, a number of cases in which people motivated by high-power religious ideology believed that they were under a divine command to perpetrate their heinous acts of violence. Even if the justification is not the same, there is a kind of family resemblance in the nature of argumentation and religious justification for violence. There are also cases in which, even if religion is not directly involved in violence and its justification, certain acts of violence like the self-infliction of death through *hara-kiri* in Japan is ritually performed. In this way, death is endowed with a sacred meaning. There is no difficulty in this regard even if the death takes place for political or economic reasons, as long as the concerned religious community confers the aura of the sacred on those acts.

2. The unambiguous

There is something which is unambiguous in the midst of much ambiguity: it is the conviction of the 'martyrs' that their death or willing self-sacrifice is for a noble cause – to defend faith, to uphold justice, to preserve the identity of a people, etc. Added to this is the belief that there is an immeasurable reward – immediate entry into heaven, a special place in paradise, total forgiveness of sins and so on. In traditional Christian understanding of martyrdom, the death was the glorification of God. Further, the martyrs are borne by the conviction that through their sacrificial death, the prevalent situation will change either within a short time, or in a distant future. The element of *life* is deeply ingrained in the ideal of martyrdom and in the mind of those who sacrifice themselves.

We can discern a certain universal pattern in the experience the martyrs undergo before their suffering. It is not one of sorrow and mourning, but of exuberant joy that dwarfs the suffering and pain inflicted upon them. In the narratives of the passion of the early Christian Perpetua, we realize what this experience means. In contemporary times similar experience has been reported about the women of Bahai faith when faced with imprisonment and torture. Marc Juergensmeyer in his recent work entitled *Terror in the Mind of God* notes how the 'suicide-bombers' before undergoing their 'self-chosen martyrdom' are filled with joy and serenity in the awareness that their death is something which will bring them face to face with God, and redeem the community in whose liberation they lay down their lives.[4]

3. Martyrdom spiritualized

Religions do not simply equate martyrdom with violent physical death. There is a process of internalization and spiritualization of the ideal. If this spiritual and interior dimension of struggle and suffering associated with martyrdom is lost, there is the danger of any religion being misunderstood. A very obvious example is the ideal of *jihad* in Islam which is basically a matter of struggle and conflict a person undergoes to combat his or her impulses and evil inclinations ('greater *jihad*'), and to strive in the way of God. This spiritual dimension present right from the time of prophet Muhammad found privileged expression and development in the Sufi tradition. In Christianity the ideal of martyrdom was spiritualized in terms of self-sacrificing and ascetic practices ('white martyrdom'). In fact, the ending of persecution and the cessation of martyrdom in the early centuries led many Christians to have recourse to the deserts for ascetic and sacrificial practices. Similarly, the battlefield which is the setting for the Hindu scripture of Bhagavad-Gita, is but a symbol of the war that is to be waged within the self and the struggles it involves. The divine Lord Krishna functioning as the charioteer carrying the warrior Arjuna to the battlefield instructs him on the need of the struggle, and how he (Arjuna) should not shy away from his duty.

Another form of spiritualization happens when martyrdom is turned into a contemplative experience as in the Kabbalist and Hasidic tradition of Judaism. One undergoes the experience of death voluntarily at a contemplative level (*Nefilat Appayim*). In Buddhism with the development of Mahayana (the wider path), the Bodhisattvas who postponed their own final state of Enlightenment till others reached that goal have been viewed as martyrs because of the self-sacrifice involved therein. The Jataka commentaries in Buddhism present to us the sacrificial deaths undergone by the Bodhisattva. In this connection we need to mention also the mythology of King Sibi shared both by Hindu and Buddhist traditions. King Sibi parted with his flesh and finally the whole of his body to be faithful to his duty as a king to protect his subjects. The prototype of Harichandra – the mythical figure who lost his all to be truthful – served as the chief inspiration for Mahatma Gandhi in his development of the ideal of martyrdom as *satyagraha* – steadfastness in truth, not counting the cost.[5]

There is a metamorphosis of martyrdom when religions try to view it as part of the cosmic war. This is another way of spiritualizing martyrdom, but with serious ambiguous consequences. Placed within the framework of cosmic war, dying and inflicting death often get justified. What is at work is a religious vision of a universal battle of the good over the evil or Satan, to end in the final triumph of the good. The cosmic war is something that has lent support to many acts of violence and killing of many innocent by religiously militant groups. The deaths caused are viewed as unfortunate but inevitable in a situation of cosmic war. Whether it is the bombing of the abortion clinics in USA, or letting out poisonous gas in the Tokyo subway, or the militant acts of Osama Bin Laden, there is lurking behind it all a view of the world in the situation of conflict and war.[6] The perception of world-situation is rife for the creation of martyrs who will sacrifice themselves for the ultimate triumph.

Speaking of the spiritualization of martyrdom, we need to underline also another process that has taken place. The interiorization and spiritualization has turned martyrdom from something belonging to exceptional individuals in a religious tradition to something that can be practised by all. From here it is only a small step to popularize the ideal of martyrdom and see the practice, for example, of *jihad* – interior and exterior – as part of Islamic religious identity.

III. Martyrdom in evolution

The conception of martyrdom has not remained the same in the course of religious history. It has been changing according to the external conditions and developments in history. In this sense we need to do also a social theorizing in respect of the conditions and circumstances – social, cultural, economic and political – which facilitate the emergence of martyrs in various religious traditions.

We note how the ideal of martyrdom is refashioned and deployed to ever new and changing circumstances. In this process there takes place often a shift of emphasis and emergence of new foci. A case in point is *jihad* which has not always remained, as often interpreted, as a war against aliens and unbelievers. Mediaeval Sufism as a contemplative movement de-emphasized physical martyrdom and focussed more on the inner spiritual struggle. Later on *jihad*, from being a high spiritual ideal, was popularized to became synonymous with the duty of every Muslim to fight unbelievers and sacrifice oneself in the process.

In Islam the traditional ideal of *jihad* and martyr (in Shi'ite tradition associated with the suffering and death of the revolutionary hero Husayn ibn 'Alis as an archetype) has found a renaissance in contemporary political activism both in relation to outside forces and those in Islam, opposed to authentic profession of faith.[7] In this process there has taken place a reconstruction of martyrdom in opposition to a too spiritualized and quietist understanding of *jihad* developed by scholars in mediaeval times under the influence of Sufism. That explains how the traditionally passive suffering servant-like image of Husyan was reworked into a politically active figure to such an extent that it could stir up the Iranian people (representing the Shi'ite tradition) to revolt against the regime of Shah in 1978, and bring it down. A re-interpretation of *jihad* in contemporary times is directed against the influence of the West and what is perceived as its ungodly and secular ways both outside and inside Islamic societies. This development has generated a new breed of martyrs in Islam.

How the external circumstances shape and mould the ideal of martyrdom can be seen also from the Jewish tradition. It appears that martyrdom as an ideal is something that came to be established much later with its beginning in the book of Esther and more fully developed in the book of Daniel. The situation before that did not lend itself for the development of the ideal and practice of martyrdom for two reasons: the absence of any connection between death with an afterlife reward, and the religious tolerance manifested by the powers that ruled over Israel. As for the Chinese, their pragmatism and love for life coupled with the values of harmony and tolerance did not create the external circumstances for extolling self-sacrificial death and martyrdom. Even then, it is a fact that there have been numerous instances in which people preferred death to succumbing to oppression and unrighteousness. The Taiping uprising and Boxer rebellion produced its own martyrs.

Mahatma Gandhi incorporated the Hindu tradition of renunciation and sacrifice into his ideal of *satyagraha* (steadfastness in truth) as a rallying point to resist and challenge the colonial government. Though Buddhism has been characterized as a religious tradition which forbids any harm or violence, we still in its history have examples of self-immolation occasioned by external circumstances, as was the case with the Buddhist monks during Vietnam war. The self-immolation of the Buddhist monk Thich Quang Duc at an intersection in Saigon on 11 June 1963 stirred up the nation to political resistance against war-mongering imperialism, and served as a powerful symbol of freedom. Here is an example of how a religiously sanctioned act of self-sacrifice confers a sacred meaning to political conflicts. There are antecedents in Buddhist religious history of such acts of self-immolation as part of a religious and spiritual quest. But the *new historical context* served the transformation of this 'martyr' ideal into a compelling political reality.

Early Christian martyrs were part of a powerless group in the Roman empire. The 'martyrs' of the Crusades, on the other hand, emerged at a time when the Western Christian powers were involved in battle. In modern times, we have innumerable martyrs who laid down their lives for their love for the poor. Further, within the Roman Catholic tradition, the shift and reworking of martyr ideal could be seen in such events as the canonization of Maria Goretti and Kolbe as martyrs, or in the general acclaim of Bishop Oscar Romero as a martyr. We have the sacrificial death of even a Catholic bishop, Bishop John Joseph of Pakistan who, confronted with an unjust state which harassed the Christians, shot himself in the court premises. Perhaps he thought that the best way to bear witness and pave the way for the future of faith in his country was to sacrifice his own self, as a sign of protest. This puzzling incident makes us think of the vast difference between the classic Christian ideal of martyrdom and its newer forms packed with political message.

Conclusion

Religions claim the prerogative to illuminate matters that are of an absolute order such as life and death. The mode of these explanations, given the mysterious nature of the realities themselves, has been in terms of symbols, myths and rituals which transcend the realm of critical reason. These forms of explanation seek to reconcile the contradictions in actual life-experience. Martyrdom is one such religious mode of explaining what appears to be humanly a tragedy. The construct of 'martyr' is something that comes out of the community which claims him or her to be someone who holds aloft to the point of death all those ideals it cherishes. In all religious traditions the ideal of martyrdom has undergone an evolution with reference to the concrete historical context. We note also in all major religious traditions an interiorization and spiritualization of martyrdom, in such a way that this ideal is made accessible to all the believers of the particular religious community.

The victimhood, pain, suffering and death associated with martyrdom are mirrored in political realities. The ideology, moods and motivations provided by religion are today transposed to the sites of ethnic, regional and national conflicts. As a result, we must face up to the serious ambiguities which surround martyrdom. As in the case of religion, the spectrum of martyrdom has become so very wide in its operation and interpretation. Martyrdom, like religion, stands for the noblest things and the most heinous crimes human beings are capable of – all in the name of God.

Religious traditions need to counterbalance the classic ideal of martyrdom with education for tolerance and peace. Today, blowing the martyr ideal out of proportion could foster religious fundamentalism and turn religions into the very opposite of what they claim to be – agents of peace. We do not need 'martyrs' of religious bigotry and obscurantism. The world today needs *witnesses* (original meaning of 'martyr') of love, justice, peace and tolerance, who will be ready to sacrifice their very selves for greater understanding among peoples, nations and religions. These martyrs will not be the possession of any one particular religious community. They will belong to the whole of humanity by reason of the fact that, through their sacrifice, steadfastness, fidelity and fortitude, they bear witness to the universal values of truth, love, justice, peace. Could the various religious traditions jointly create the climate for the emergence of such universal martyrs? It involves rethinking martyrdom, and that is where we need to begin.

Notes

1. Cf. Peter Raj Perianayagam, *Soldiers of Christ. A Study of the Military Martyrs with Special Reference to the Acts of Maximilian,* Catholic University of Louvain, Louvain 1993.
2. Cf. Arthur Kleinman, Veena Das, Margaret Lock (eds), *Social Suffering*, Oxford University Press, Delhi 1998.
3. Cf. René Girard, *Violence and the Sacred*, John Hopkins University Press, Baltimore 1977; id., *The Scapegoat*, John Hopkins University Press, Baltimore 1986.
4. Mark Juergensmeyer, *Terror in the Mind of God*, University of California Press, Berkeley 2001, pp. 72ff.
5. Cf. Dennis Hudson, 'Self-Sacrifice as Truth in India' in Margaret Cormack (ed), *Sacrificing the Self. Perspectives on Martyrdom and Religion*, Oxford University Press, NewYork 2002, pp. 132–52.
6. Mark Juergensmeyer, op.cit., pp. 145ff.
7. Daniel Brown, 'Martyrdom in Sunni Revivalist Thought' in Margeret Cormack (ed), op.cit., pp. 107–17; Keith Lewinstein, 'The Revaluation of Martyrdom in Ealry Islam', ibid., pp. 78–91.

III. The Problem of Martyrdom in the Religions

The Problem of Martyrdom in Missionary Countries

GEORG EVERS

In the theology of mission, which is relatively new as a theological discipline, there are not many discussions of 'martyrdom and mission'. This is quite amazing when we consider the large number of witnesses to the faith in the missionary countries, above all in Asia. Thus while the *Lexikon Missionstheologischer Grundbegriffe*[1] has an article on martyrdom, it is exclusively limited to the martyrs of the early church. On the other hand it is true that 'mission and martyrdom belong together. Martyrdom is especially at home on the mission field.'[2] The history of missions down to our day indicates that missionaries have always understood themselves as messengers of the good and liberating news of Jesus Christ which has to be proclaimed everywhere, 'in season and out of season' (cf. II Tim.4.2), even at the cost of one's life. Missionaries have also required similar resolution and steadfastness of those who have become Christians as a result of their preaching, when there has been persecution of the church and faith. Missionaries have never felt that the prohibitions issued by governments in missionary countries and the legal banning of Christianity applied to them. 'There are no closed lands if you do not expect to return.'[3] This is an expression of a missionary awareness of being sent to preach the message in all circumstances. Where a land seems closed because the rulers prohibit preaching, there is no holding back for missionaries, at any rate not if they are prepared for martyrdom.

I. Martyrs 'for the faith'

According to church tradition martyrs are those who take upon themselves death 'for the sake of the faith' (*in odium fidei*) passively, i.e. not actively or militantly.[4] Karl Rahner argued for an extension of the concept of martyrdom because in the conditions of our time the persecutors of Christianity and their methods have changed a great deal.[5] Here he was concerned also to recognize as martyrs those who gave their lives in the fight for justice and other Christian values.⁶ But martyrdom in our day tends more to be hidden martyrdom, which in view of modern forms of brainwashing and torture often consists in someone like Cardinal Mindszenty standing before the judges a broken man, incapable of giving a glorious testimony of unbroken courage and faith. We find something similar with Dries van Coillie, missionary to China, who has given an impressive description of his experiences of brainwashing in China at the beginning of the 1950s. Even though he steadfastly survived the long weeks of brainwashing, deep wounds and uncertainties remained which made him feel that his own testimony was in some way broken and polluted – and not at all radiant heroism.⁷ In this form of martyrdom the whole personality of an individual is annihilated and he or she is no longer given even the possibility of defending their convictions of their own free will. The years in prisons and labour camps endured by many Chinese bishops, priests and faithful – the same is true of the church in Vietnam – fulfil this state of 'inglorious' martyrdom which is all the more difficult to bear.

On the other hand, martyrdom is always something that is sent. It is not something that one seizes for oneself, or for which one simply reports and into which one forces one's way. Things are different in other religious traditions. In Buddhism a positive view is taken of the self-immolations of Buddhist monks and nuns of the kind that took place, for example, in Vietnam some decades ago, as actions in conformity with the Buddhist tradition. In recent years the concept of martyrdom has been vigorously discussed inside and outside Islam as a result of the growing number of Muslim suicide bombers; however, it has also fallen into disrepute because here the perpetrators are not only sacrificing their own lives but also deliberately intending the deaths of others. The scriptural statement 'Did not the messiah have to suffer and thus enter into his glory?' (Luke 24.26) makes it clear that martyrdom has a firm place in salvation history. However, it is illegitimate to conclude from this that martyrdom is to be aimed at always and everywhere. The readiness of, for example, nineteenth-century missionaries for martyrdom was expressed in a way which must be regarded as exaggerated and unhealthy.

If we read the farewell letters of missionaries who set off for Vietnam, China or Korea at the time, we find in them almost stereotyped expressions of an ardent desire to be thought worthy of martyrdom, to be able to shed their 'blood as the seed for the growth of the church'. This longing for martyrdom is bound up with a conviction that opponents and enemies will

The Problem of Martyrdom in Missionary Countries 89

be found in the governments and religions of these lands who out of false religious and ethical convictions will maliciously do all that they can to prevent the proclamation of the Christian message. This negative attitude to the predominant cultural, religious and philosophical ideas in these countries rested less on actual knowledge than on condemnations which had been issued, for example, in the Rites Dispute, had been taken over unquestioned, and afterwards might no longer be investigated and discussed.

II. The churches of Asia – churches of the martyrs

The most prominent characteristic of the churches of Asia is that they can look back on a great many martyrs. That is true of the churches in Japan, Vietnam, Korea, China and many other Asian countries. There are said to have been 125,000 martyrs in Vietnam in the nineteenth century alone. In China more than 30,000 Catholics were killed for their faith during the Boxer rebellion in 1900. The persecutions of the Chinese Catholics in the years after the establishment of the People's Republic of China which came to a climax in the Cultural Revolution (1966–76) claimed thousands more victims. In the seventeenth century the Japanese Christians showed that despite severe torture by the state authorities, thousands of them could hold fast to the faith, and paid for this with their lives. It was and is the pride of the Vietnamese church that it is a 'church of martyrs'. In the period between 1625 and 1776 alone there are said to have been 130,000 Christian victims of persecution. The Korean church similarly understands itself to be a 'church of martyrs', which despite the deaths of hundreds of witnesses to the faith has continued to survive underground. The beatifications and canonizations of these martyrs in Korea, Vietnam and China have therefore also always taken place as a celebration of remembrance and the expression of an abiding commitment to prove worthy of this heritage. At the same time they have always also been the occasion to look at this heritage with pride and to praise the power of God's grace. If we familiarize ourselves with the reports of the life and death of these witnesses we can only wonder at the steadfastness of these women, men and even children, and the strength of their faith.

1. The beatification of Vietnamese and Chinese martyrs – a controversy

When in Rome on 19 June 1988 Pope John Paul II beatified 117 Vietnamese martyrs who had given their lives as witnesses to the faith between 1745 and

1862, this met with vigorous opposition from the Communist government of Vietnam, who saw it as a slur on the governments of the time. In an official communiqué it stated that it regarded the proceedings of the feudal rulers of the time against foreign missionaries and their Vietnamese accomplices as quite justified and necessary. Moreover these new Vietnamese saints also included people who had perpetrated criminal acts like treachery against their homeland and had therefore rightly been executed. The glorification of these 'minions of the colonialists' as 'saints' was, they claimed, an insult to the honour of the whole Vietnamese people.

The Chinese government protested with almost identical arguments when on 1 August 2000 Pope John Paul II beatified 120 martyrs who had suffered martyrdom in the period between the seventeenth century and the Boxer rebellion in 1900. Despite all the assertions on the part of the Vatican that the beatification of the Chinese martyrs was a ceremony with a purely religious character, the Chinese government saw it as deliberate provocation which, as an official protest note put it, represented 'yet another violation of the feelings of the Chinese people'. In the past, the note stated, the Christian missionaries had 'collaborated with the forces of colonialism and imperialism and profited from the unjust treaties'. Again individual beatified foreign missionaries and Chinese Christians were accused of not having been 'holy' in their way of life; they were said to have committed serious crimes. In the case of both the Vietnamese and the Chinese martyrs the Vatican carefully avoided including martyrs who had lost their lives under Communist rule after 1949.

2. Pride in the martyrs – and silence about the apostates?

In the 1960s the Japanese Catholic writer Shusaku Endo caused great offence in Japan with his book *Silence*, which achieved public notoriety. The book was about the persecution of the Japanese Christians at the beginning of the seventeenth century. Endo was one of the first to draw attention to the discrepancy between the pride which the Catholic Church shows in 'its martyrs' and its silence over Christians who did not withstand persecutions and apostatized from the faith. Is this silence justified because the church cannot recognize members who were not prepared to go the way of the cross to the end? Is the way of the martyrs always the right one? To put it sharply, were the situations in which Christians in Japan, to keep to the Japanese martyrs, found themselves so clear that there was no other possibility of being a true Christian than martyrdom? Was faith really so clearly at stake in the controversy? What was the significance of their 'failure'? Is only the tradition of glorious testimony important, or is there not also a power in the brokenness of failure and betrayal – the power which comes from weakness (cf. II Cor.12.9)?

3. Why was Christianity persecuted in Asia?

A look at the mission history of the Asian churches makes one think. On the one hand there is the fact that the churches of Japan, Korea, China and Japan are rightly proud of their many martyrs. But in Asia the question also arises in connection with the Rites Dispute: did the decisions of the church really have to be so harsh and negative? And connected with that: was there really no alternative for the many martyrs who willingly gave their lives on the basis of these decisions? The question arises in yet another way if we change the perspective and ask ourselves why the governments in Japan, in Vietnam, in Korea and in China dealt with Christians in such a cruel way. Was it in each case the result of a 'hatred of religion (*odium fidei*), of God, of the gospel of Jesus Christ' – the attributes which canonically and theologically are normally mentioned as the presuppositions for martyrdom?

Generally speaking the main reason for the persecutions of Christians in Japan, Korea, Vietnam and China may be said to be their rejection of ancestor worship, which in the negative decisions of the Roman authorities was described as an 'ancestor cult' and thus condemned as being incompatible with the Christian faith. The controversies in the so-called Rites Dispute over the question whether the veneration of ancestors and of Confucius in China, Korea, Japan and Vietnam were traditional customs, which predominantly had a civil character and only at a secondary level a religious character, have become centrally important in the missionary history of East Asia. The negative decision of Rome, which claimed that these 'rites' had a religious character and therefore were incompatible with Christian faith, resulted in Asian Christians becoming outsiders in their societies. In the controversies over the Rites Dispute the Catholic church authorities in Rome adopted positions which ruled out any compromise and forbade Catholics to take part in any way in the veneration of ancestors and expressions of reverence for Confucius: this was held to be idolatry.

The reactions of the governments in China, Japan, Korea and Vietnam were everywhere the same. This attitude of Christians was regarded as subversive, because it put in question important elements of the existing social system. Moreover the fact that the indigenous Christians were subject to instructions from abroad, i.e. from the headquarters in Rome, on such important questions was regarded as 'interference in the internal affairs' of the countries concerned and condemned. The often very close collaboration between the European colonial powers and the Christian mission often had a negative effect. In quite a few cases the protection of Christian missionaries and their converts was used by European governments as a pretext for military intervention and the extension of colonies.

It is worth taking a critical look at the history of colonization, e.g. in Vietnam. Here the persecution of Christians played a not inconsiderable role. France, in the homeland a strictly lay country, appeared in Vietnam as the defender of the Christian West and the Christian mission – yet in doing so was essentially pursuing only its own power-political interests. The role which France assumed as the guardian of the Christian mission in China was similar. In the history of Korean mission and the Korean church there is a case which has inscribed itself deeply on the collective consciousness of the Koreans: Catholic Christians sent a petition to the French government asking for military intervention against their own government in order to protect the Christians in Korea.

Here two attitudes are fundamentally opposed. The authorities in Asia banned and suppressed Christianity as a 'false religion'. Over against these measures by governments stood the attitude of the foreign missionaries, who appealed to a 'divine right' to preach the gospel and therefore thought that they need not respect the ordinances of the local state authorities. They regarded laws against them as 'the machinations of the devil' and a hindrance to the proclamation of the word of God. Then the 'pagan' rulers always appeared as godless tyrants, who opposed God out of corruption and sinfulness.

III. Martyrdom today

1. *Papal confessions of guilt*

Pope John Paul II is the first pope in church history officially to have conceded that individual missionaries in the history of the church acted wrongly out of a failure to respect cultural and religious traditions and went too far in their collaboration with the colonial powers. This concession was made for the first time at the beginning of Lent in the Holy Year 2000 and attracted great attention and recognition all over the world. In his request for forgiveness the pope said that Christians 'have used words and adopted attitudes which were full of pride, which were stamped by hatred and governed by the desire to dominate others, and which showed enmity to the members of other religions'. Putting this the other way round, we can ask how far these attitudes were not also the catalyst for the persecution and 'martyrdom' of Christians. For in the end here Christians were 'violating the rights of ethnic groups and showing contempt for their cultures and religions', as the pope goes on to say. On October 2001, in his address on the 400th anniversary of the coming of Matteo Ricci to Beijing, the pope conceded a second time that missionaries in the past had lacked respect for other cultures and religions and also apologized for errors of the Catholic Church which had been committed in the course of missionary history. In particular he mentioned the false attitude of some missionaries who had violated the feelings of the Chinese people by being too closely associated with the colonial powers and by their lack of respect for Chinese culture.

2. Martyrdom for justice and understanding between religions?

There are new forms of Christian proclamation and testimony which consist in commitment to social justice and understanding between the religions. In particular in recent decades there has been a series of martyrs in this connection, in Asia, Africa and Latin America. In India, Christians from all churches have condemned the caste systems, which gives religious legitimation to a social evil that poisons the whole of Indian society. The fight against the injustices of the caste system can be seen as a prophetic challenge by Christians in India. If in this controversy they become victims of persecution, this testimony to justice can be seen as a testimony to true discipleship and thus as genuine martyrdom. The example of Bishop Oscar Romero in San Salvador has shown that there is a form of martyrdom which is convincing because it is based on 'God's preferential option for the poor': giving one's life for them is in fact a testimony to God's purposes in this world. Similarly, in San Salvador there was the testimony of the six Jesuits around José Ellacuría and the two women who were murdered on 16 November 1989 by right-wing soldiers on the campus of the University of Central America.[8] They too died because they took the side of the poor and paid for their option for the poor with their lives.

The testimony of the life and death of Michael Rodrigo, OMI, in Sri Lanka also stands in this context. He took new ways in Christian-Buddhist dialogue by giving an example of Christian presence among the Buddhist rural population in the small locality of Buttala. At the same time he fought resolutely for the rights of the poor against exploitation by the rich landowners. Despite massive threats from the landowners, together with the women who worked with him he refused to stop his championing of the rights of poor people and withdraw from Buttala, as he was ordered. On 10 November 1987 he was shot at the altar at the end of a mass. Michael Rodrigo is one example of many other Christians in Asia who have lost their life in the fight for social justice and in commitment to interfaith dialogue. Fr Salvatore Carzedda, PIME, can also be seen as a martyr in interfaith dialogue. With his brother religious Sebastiano D'Ambra he had been an active leader in the Silsilah dialogue movement in Zamboanga. His murder on 20 May 1992 was the reaction of radical Islamicist circles, who saw the peace work of the Silsilah movement as merely a danger and a threat to their own politics, which was based on violence. The Trappists of Thibirine in Algeria, who were first abducted by Muslim fighters and then cruelly murdered on 26 May 1996, can likewise be seen as martyrs in interfaith dialogue. The prior, Christian de Chergé, had made the monastery a centre of Christian-Muslim dialogue. Despite many threats the monks had refused to leave their monastery and resolved to remain and continue their efforts for dialogue.

IV. Between collaboration and confession – the example of China

Reports about the Catholic Church in the People's Republic of China usually speak of a divided church and make a distinction between the 'official church', which to some degree works with the state authorities, and the 'underground church', which refuses any form of co-operation and is therefore exposed to much harassment and persecution. Cardinal Gong Pinmei (1901–2000), who spent almost thirty years in prison or labour camps and died in exile in the USA, is an example of this uncompromising position. By contrast, the position of the bishops and priests who are ready in various way to co-operate with the state authorities is more difficult and more inglorious. At what point does 'limited collaboration' become a betrayal of fundamental principles? Does the right of the pope to nominate bishops, for example, stand on the same level as the obligation to work for justice to the poor? Has not a 'hierarchy of truths' also to be noted in these questions? The rejection of any kind of collaboration with state authorities within the underground church is often based on a reduction of faith to a few theological principles, which in other circumstances would be regarded as bigotry and a lack of intelligence. After all, it is often the case that 'resolution' is not only to be attributed to those inspired by supreme virtues; a resolute person may simply be incapable of taking into account other perspectives which would necessarily lead to an essentially more nuanced attitude. Specifically, for example in the history of the persecution of the Catholic Church in the People's Republic of China, not all collaboration with the Communist Party and its political apparatus need amount to a betrayal of Catholic principles. More reflective types find it difficult to make such unequivocal statements. With their more differentiated attitude they easily fall under suspicion of lacking resolution and making too many compromises. Then boundaries become fluid and individual decisions questionable, and with hindsight can possibly even prove false.

There is a degree of tragedy here. Those who have made compromises easily fall between all the stools. They are often despised by the state authorities with which they collaborate and are taunted and likewise despised as collaborators within their own community.

Translated by John Bowden

Notes

1. 'Martyrium', *Lexikon Missionstheologischer Grundbegriffe*, ed K. Müller and T. Sundermeier, Berlin 1987, pp. 266–70.
2. Hans von Campenhausen, *Das Martyrium in der Mission*, Frohne & Knorr 1974, p. 71.
3. Lary Poston, Evangelical Missiological Society National Meeting, 15 November 2000.
4. In this issue see the article by G. Faust, 'Witnesses to Love, Killed by Hatred of Love'.
5. In this issue see the introductions to the articles by G. Faust and S. J. Emmanuel.
6. 'The modern "persecutors of Christians" will not give today's Christians any chance at all to confess their faith in the way it was done in the first Christian centuries and to accept the death which the tribunal decrees for them. Yet death in the more anonymous forms of modern persecution may be foreseen and accepted as it was by the ancient martyrs. And this death can be a consequence of an active struggle for justice and other Christian values,' Karl Rahner, 'Dimensions of Martyrdom', in *Theological Investigations* 22, New York and London 1992, p. 111.
7. Cf. Dries van Coillie, *Der begeisterte Selbstmord*, Freiburg 1965.
8. J. Sobrino, I. Ellacuría et al., *Companions of Jesus, The Jesuit Martyrs of El Salvador*, Maryknoll 1990.

Christians' Responsibility in Situations of Violence: A Challenge for Churches

PETER KANYANDAGO

Introduction: theoretical remarks

It is not common to associate Christians with violence, although Christians in many ways recognize and confess their sinfulness. In the Catholic Church however, Pope John Paul II's public demand for pardon on 12 March 2002 for sins committed by the daughters and sons of the church has shown that a church can, with humility and courage, accept officially its sinfulness. The main purpose of this contribution is to highlight the responsibility of Christians in situations of violence without implying that Christians have the monopoly of this evil. My starting point is that Christians have promoted, perpetrated and justified violence. What is astonishing is that the churches are virtually silent about this. I will refer specifically to Western Christianity in as far as it has had organized systems of evangelizing. I will also try to identify the root causes of the violence it sometimes perpetrates or promotes. Evangelization has often gone hand in hand with the aggressive cultural process and practices of Westernization which has tried to make the whole world look like the West.[1] We can appreciate the importance of this if we realize that by 1900, European/US colonial powers controlled the following percentages of the mentioned regions of the world: Africa (90.4%), Polynesia (98.9%), Asia (56.5%), Australia (100%),and Americas (27.2%);[2] that is, 75% of the world had by then been brought under the control of Western powers. We also know that this control was brought about by using violent means and ideologies including genocides in the Americas, Australia and Africa, the slave trade,the looting of natural resources and the use of racism.

In this process, one can identify some interconnected practices and ideologies which promote violence. There is denial of the other based on the Western claim that their civilization is superior in the hierarchy of races. This was supported by the Christian racist doctrine based on the Hamitic myth positing that the Black race was cursed to be slaves by Noah through

Ham and his son.³ Pope Pius XI attached an indulgence to prayers for the 'wretched Ethiopians in Central Africa' that the 'Almighty God may at length remove the curse of Cham [Ham] from their hearts'.⁴ To these one should add the economic system of capitalism which has now assumed global importance with its attendant problems for humanity and the environment from the time its bases were put in place when Western explorers set out to look for resources outside Europe towards the end of the fifteenth century. Then there is the whole issue of how power is used in institutions. Its abuse, mainly by men, to ensure that a few control it in order to have access to resources leads to violence in civil and church institutions. The points above are to be considered against the background of the world-view and culture that produces them. Christianity can change negative cultural practices because culture is dynamic, and so there is need to create a critical interface between culture and theology. Theological discourse therefore is grounded in a given anthropological context with its values and non-values which influence theology and Christian practices. I believe that by recognizing that Christians also contribute towards violence as victimizers, this will help us to situate martyrdom in a better perspective. My analysis will extend to areas which have undergone Western influence and Christianity.

I. Violence against non-Europeans and non-Christians

Towards the end of fifteenth century Portugal and Spain, sometimes supported by papal bulls, pioneered slave trade, genocides, colonization and violent seizure of resources of other people. They were later joined by the other Western countries in this worst form of violence that humanity has known. Although the churches were not involved directly, they gave theological justifications to some of the forms of this violence. Let us look at some Christian justifications of this violence.

1. Pope Nicholas V on slave trade and colonization

On 18 June 1452, Pope Nicholas V issued the bull *Dum Diversas* authorizing the king of Portugal to subdue pagans and other non-believers. This was followed by his bull *Romanus Pontifex* on 8 January 1455 reinforcing what had been said in the previous bull. The pope bestows upon the Catholic kings and princes the powers and benefits they need to conquer other lands and convert pagans to Christianity and to reduce the Saracens (Black Africans) to perpetual slavery. The bull does not only authorize the king of Portugal 'to invade, search out, capture, vanquish, and subdue all Saracens and pagans whatsoever' but also to subdue all 'other enemies of Christ wheresoever placed', thus including all people who were not Christians. We know that the native Americans received a rough treatment at the hands of the colonizers.[5] What is disturbing is that the church has not revoked these documents and Western theology has been practically silent about this violence against people who were not European and Christian.

Colonizers and evangelizers agreed on the presumption that the West had a mission to 'civilize' what they saw as retarded or savage people. We know that some popes and individual Christians and organizations wrote and fought against the slave trade, but one finds little trace of condemnation of colonization, but rather its justification by one of the theologians.

2. Albert Muller's doctrine on colonization

If we come nearer to our era, we find a Belgian Jesuit, Albert Muller, who published a book in 1927 giving Christian principles to justify colonization. Written at a time when the scramble for Africa and its division between the major European powers was almost complete, Muller deplores the absence of Christian theology on colonization. His starting point is not to question colonization but to defend it using Christian morality based on revelation and on the teaching of the church.[6] He goes on to develop what he considers to be the essential points of the Catholic doctrine of colonization.[7] For him, colonization is 'the taking possession of territories occupied by societies of an inferior culture by the colonizing nation'.[8] He argues that world resources are intended for the satisfaction of the needs of all people but that 'retarded people' are not able to use properly what they possess.

> Humanity ought not, cannot accept that the incapacity, negligence and laziness of the savage people leave without use indefinitely the riches which God has entrusted to them with the mission to make them serve the good of all people. If there happen to be territories which are badly administered by their lawful proprietors, it is the right of the societies which are wronged by this defective stewardship to take the place of these incapable stewards and to exploit the goods they do not put to good use for the benefit of all people.[9]

Colonization is for the benefit of the colonized 'small tribes'[10] since

> ... the savage and debased people, victims of vice, of ignorance and super-

stition, cannot elevate themselves by their own resources above the quagmire where they are wallowing.[11]

On the issue of violence used by colonizers, Muller exonerates them by saying that even if there are 'faults and crimes at the origin of colonization, one should observe that the colonial enterprises have definitely brought to the subjugated people more benefits than the harm done to them'.[12]

Colonization which brought untold suffering to the colonized, with its effects still affecting former colonies, is said to fulfil a divine mission. This attitude has not basically changed. From this we can see that there is little difference between the anthropological views that inspired *Romanus Pontifex* in the fifteenth century, Muller in the twentieth century and the pronouncements of Western leaders today claiming that they are the champions of justice and democracy.

II. Christians and violence in the Americas

Let us now look at some situations of violence and how Christians are involved in them. If we take the case of the Americas, the extermination of the native Americans in North, Central and Central America by the colonizers beginning from 1492 was done by Christians from Europe. Estimates of people who were killed using torture, starvation, forced labour, disease are put at tens of millions, and killings of these people have been continued by foreigners who want to use land occupied by the American natives.[13] It is surprising that Liberation Theology has not devoted much theological reflection to this violence. The struggle of the Zapatistas guerrilla movement in the Chiapaz state in Mexico for autonomy could be an indication of how these people have been brutally suppressed.

1. *Disappearing people*

Since evangelization and colonization by the Spaniards and Portuguese, Latin America is one of the areas with the highest numbers of Catholics. Besides the violence against American natives mentioned above, Latin America has passed through a period of violence and political upheaval which have pushed Christians and non-Christians to look for solutions. If one can speak of a land of martyrdom, then Latin America qualifies. The victimizers have been mainly Christian governments, and in some cases the churches have been accused of complicity with politicians. Many people have disappeared to join those who have now come to be known as the *'desaparecidos'*. Some liberation groups have espoused revolutionary and violent means to bring about changes. However, this has made some church leaders to fear the use of violence and Marxist ideology. It is in this kind of atmosphere that Liberation Theology came to birth with emphasis on the importance basic ecclesial communities, political dimension of faith, due attention to be paid to history, critical reflection upon praxis, use of Marxist analysis and a preferential option for the poor.[14] It is also known that there are tensions in the Latin American Episcopal Conference showing divisions between the bishops who are seen as conservatives and the others as progressives. This has not prevented them from organizing two very important general conferences, one in 1968 at Medellín, Colombia, and another in 1979, at Puebla, which have marked significantly the life of the church in that region. Economic violence has also been the order of the day. In most cases, violence was perpetrated by governments of Christian leaders.

2. Chile

In Chile, in 1970 the election of Salvador Allende to a socialist government had brought some hopes but in 1973 he was overthrown by a military junta led by Pinochet, and was murdered with the support of the American government.[15] Later the military junta defined its objectives saying that 'the regime is inspired by Christian principles and identifies exclusively with 'Christian Western civilization'''.[16]

3. El Salvador

Some Church leaders have openly supported the cause of the poor who are looking for liberation. In El Salvador, Archbishop Oscar Armulfo Romero supported the poor and was assassinated on 24 March 1980. In the same year eight leftist politicians, three American nuns and a lay worker, to mention those who have been written about, were killed. On 16 November 1989, six Jesuits who were teaching at the University of Central America were gunned down with their cook and her daughter.[17] This took place when the Marxist group Farabundo Marti National Liberation Front had launched an attack on the city. Many people lost their lives in this attack. In this case the church and its leaders were a direct target by a Christian government.

4. Nicaragua

Responses to violence in the church in Nicaragua offer some points of an ecclesiological nature. The Nicaraguan Marxist revolution which toppled the Anastazio Somoza dictatorship in 1979 was supported by Christians and was seen as an opportunity where Marxists and Christians could work together to defend the rights of the poor. However, because of a combination of circumstances, the influence of what Philip Williams calls the 'progressive church' has declined within the institutional church.[18] The progressive church aiming at building a grass-roots church has not been well viewed by the hierarchy, which saw it as opposed to its authority. The action of the priests who joined the government[19] and the many other priests and religious who collaborated with the Sandinista National Liberation Front (FSLN) aggravated the situation. This led to internal and Vatican pressure being put on them so as to stop them from supporting what was seen as a parallel popular church. This has led to a conflict within the church and after the Sandinistas lost elections to the opposition in 1990, the progressive church was faced with even more challenges from within and outside the church. What is noteworthy is that the church as a whole supported the actions of a Marxist revolution for promoting gospel values. The experience of the Nicaraguan church, which of course has to be evaluated on a longer term, shows that ecclesiologically, at least in principle, the church can work with people and governments which are not necessarily 'Christian' to promote the values of the reign of God.

In Latin America it is evident that victimizers and victims of violence are Christians, coupled with external interference from the USA. Some church leaders supported liberation of the poor and others feared that the power and control of the church would be compromised and therefore attacked those who were seen as troublemakers.

III. Christians and situations of violence in Africa

1. The apartheid system

In the case of Africa, I will limit myself to two examples which show how Christians perpetrated violence. The apartheid system which was officially institutionalized in South Africa in 1948 was based on an error that according to the Bible the Whites are superior to the Blacks. The Dutch Reformed Church (Nederduitse Gereformeerde Kerk or NGK) in South Africa supported and practised the apartheid system.[20] The racist ideology was linked to an economic policy aimed at maintaining the Whites' control over resources. The effects of this demoniac system extended to neighbouring countries. It was for a long time supported by the governments and companies of Western Christian countries for economic reasons. Besides the economic violence, one has to consider the cultural violence against the races which were discriminated against.

2. Rwanda

Another case of Christians being accused of promoting violence is the Rwandese genocide of 1994 in which about one million people, mainly Tutsi, were killed. This genocide once more took place in a country which is very Christian. Emotions and passions rise when people try to explain causes of this genocide, which cannot be understood without referring to the history and cultures of that country. Most serious analyses reject the simplistic explanation of the Bahutu-Batutsi antagonism to explain the ethnic conflict. Tharcisse Gatwa, a Rwandese himself, rejects several mythology-histories to explain the ethnic conflict.[21] He sees as insufficient the explanation which presents the ethnic conflict as a product of colonization.[22] Gatwa defends the idea that

> ... the ethnic rivalry has been installed and systematized in the different mechanisms of the feudal-monarchical, colonial and missionary periods. In no case therefore should one see the social, cultural and political relations among the Banyarwanda as being fundamentally marked by the ethnic rivalry outside the influence of the three categories of actors, namely the colonialists, missionaries, and the local élites . . .[23]

Court cases against some church leaders have brought to the fore how the Christians got involved in the genocide. Bishop Augustin Misago of Gikongoro diocese was arrested on seven charges of genocide and crimes against humanity. He was kept in prison for twenty-six months and was finally acquitted in June 2000. Some analysts claim the influence of government and of local church and Vatican appeals influenced the decision.[24] Two Benedictine nuns, Sisters Gertrude and Kizito, were sentenced with two others and received sentences ranging from twelve to twenty years.[25] Mahmood Mamdani in his book with the suggestive title *When Victims Become Killers* has damning statements about the role of the Church in the genocide.

Herein lies the clue as to why the violence was marked by a greater fury in the Church than in the other institution in Rwandan society. The Church was the original ethnographer of Rwanda. It was the original author of the Hamitic hypothesis . . . After all, but for the army and the Church, the two prime movers . . . one located in the state and the other in society, there would have been no genocide.[26]

Conclusion and some theological questions

As a conclusion, let us briefly refer to some of the issues I raised in the beginning. We have seen that violence by Christians is rooted in a struggle to control and monopolize resources, which sometimes goes with the elimination of people who are seen to stand in the way of the powerful. The capitalist economic system, which has become dominant, but is not necessarily ethically the right system, is reinforced by individualism and needs to be theologically appraised. The church has been much less critical of it than of socialism. The teaching on the sharing of resources should be implemented to correct imbalances which produce violence. Claims by Westerners to be a superior civilization have produced a racism that has produced other forms of violence which have sometimes been legitimized by Christianity. Christian teaching on the equality of people, since we are all created in God's image, loses credibility if racism is not fought against in the world. Christianity teaches that life is to be respected, and Christians, especially in Europe, have committed genocides on a large scale, without even having the courage to recognize this. Abuse of power has also been identified as one of the root causes of violence. The violence by Christians which we looked at has its roots mainly in the Western world-view. Christianity must change these views if it is to remain faithful to the message of Christ. To bring about healing in the world where violence has become pervasive, we need more gestures of apology. These have to be accompanied by reparations if they are to have more significance. The body of Christ is composed of a diversity of cultures which should be celebrated instead of being feared.

Notes

1. The term West is herein used with its cultural and economic connotation, covering not only Western Europe, but also North America, Australia and New Zealand without implying that what is said applies to all Westerners.
2. Cf. http://www.mtholyoke.edu/acad/intrel/po1116/colonies.htm
3. The curse of Noah is derived from a misinterpretation of Gen. 9.20–25.

4. http://www.religioustolerance.org/chr_slav2.htm The same view is defended by a Superior of a mission, Horner, in *Voyage à la côte orientale d'Afrique* (Journey to the eastern coast of Africa), Paris: Gaume Frères et J. Duprey, 1872, pp. 1–2.
5. A translation of the bull *Romanus Pontifex* of Nicholas V, 8 January 1455 can be found on http://www.nativeweb.org/pages/legal/indig-romanus-pontifex.html
6. Albert Muller, *Principes chrétiens et colonisation*, Bruxelles: Editions de Cité Chrétienne, 1927, p. 7.
7. Ibid., p. 9.
8. Ibid., p. 9.
9. Ibid., p. 17.
10. Ibid., p. 17. 'Small tribes' is an attempt to translate the French term 'peuplades' which means groups of people with little importance in a primitive society. The use of the word denotes that such people are lesser people. Nowadays the West does not use 'small tribes' but 'ethnic groups' which also denies non-Westerners full human cultural rights.
11. Ibid., p. 19.
12. Ibid., p. 20.
13. See http://www.religioustolerance.org/genocide2.htm See same site for information on extermination of the Aboriginals of Australia.
14. See Alfred T. Hennelly (ed), *Liberation Theology: A Documentary History*, Maryknoll, New York: Orbis Books 1990, which presents some key documents about this struggle.
15. Ibid., p. 124.
16. See http://www.lakota.clara.net/derechos/chrono.htm
17. See http://www.creighton.edu/CollaborativeMinistry/WPnov16.html The six Jesuits were: Ignacio Ellacuría, Ignacio Martin-Baro, Segundo Montes, Arnando Lopez, Joaquin Lopez y Lopez and Juan Ramon Moreno. Their cook was Julia Elba Ramos and her daughter, Cecilia Ramos.
18. See his article Philip Williams, 'The Limits of Religious Influence: the Progressive Church in Nicaragua' on http://www.dominicans.org/~ecleary/conflict/conlicto7.htm The points that follow are summarized from this site.
19. The names of these priests are: Fernando Cardenal, a Jesuit; Ernest Cardenal, a Trappist; Miguel d'Escoto, a Trappist; and Edgar Parrales, a Maryknoller.
20. Finally, the Dutch Reformed Church which had been suspended from the World Alliance of Reformed Churches for sixteen years was re-admitted into the Alliance on 19 October 1998 after the Church had accepted that apartheid was a sin. See http://www.warc.ch/1998/index.html
21. See his Tharcisse Gatwa, *Rwanda, Eglises: Victimes ou coupables? Les Eglises et l'idéologie ethnique au Rwanda 1900–1994* (Rwanda, Churches: Victims or

Guilty? The Churches and the Ethnic Ideology in Rwanda 1900–1994), Yaoundé: Editions CLE 2001.
22. Ibid., p. 41.
23. Ibid., p. 43.
24. See http://www.christianitytoday.com/ct/2001/125/23.0.html
25. See http://www.hirondelle.org/hirondell . . . 655dbe9da551e5fec1256a6900427e7?OpenDocumen
26. Mahmood Mamdani, *When Victims Become Killers: Colonialism, Nativism, and the Genocide in Rwanda*, Princeton: Princeton University Press 2001, pp. 232–33.

Suffering Because of the Church: A Key Issue for Contemporary Catholicism

ALBERTO MELLONI

The problem of how the suffering endured within the church – punishment, medicine, injustice – can be justified is still almost completely unrecognized from a historical perspective. Certainly there is a knowledge of what has happened to those whom the church has condemned within the Christian regime and those on whom it has inflicted canonical penalties, but there has been little investigation and even less reflection on the way in which it has produced a mentality which thought it just to suffer as a result of the church, and how this has been dispelled. This short article does not aim at completeness: it is limited to investigating a chronological segment, that of the twentieth century, which is not necessarily the most significant; it deals particularly with a 'discipline', that of the theologians, who have not necessarily paid the highest price. It examines the way in which the suffering experienced in the church (which can be defined as 'martyrdom' only in a very figurative sense) has been profoundly changed. The method used here is that of a series of brief cameos, but this is not to suggest that the simple eloquence of an episode contains more truth than the complexity of reality: these cameos simply identify topics which will be explored elsewhere and in a different way.

I. The church of the condemnations

'We live in difficult times: they are times in which it is not enough just to "suffer for the church"; it is necessary also to "suffer as a result of the church".' This was the comment made by the Archbishop of Milan, Mgr Giovanni Battista Montini, on the situation of Jacques Maritain and of the Catholic Church in the middle 1950s.[1] The comment was by no means an isolated one at that bitter moment, and with marked resignation it diagnosed the outcome of the mistrust of freedom of theological research shown in the post-war period by Pius XII and put into practice by some of the officials and cardinals of the Roman Curia who were closest to him.[2] Thanks to them, some Roman congregations (the Holy Office, the Consistorial Congregation or the Congregation for the Seminaries) were in fact engaged in a permanent campaign of 'theological cleansing' aimed at those who were thought hostile to the faith, along with those Catholics who wanted to practise their discipline fully and deeply, but whom the ecclesiastical authorities judged to be dangerous threats to the purity of the faith.[3]

The dignitaries and churchmen who were in favour of such severity were following a line – that of condemnations – which had a tradition in the long history of the church. Basically, from the earliest excommunications to the anathemas of the great councils,[4] from the first canonical collections to the sophisticated reflections of the mediaeval decrees, we have a scarlet thread of condemnations and punishments devised and carried out in order to eradicate heresy and protect customs.[5] In some circumstances the heretic had to be tortured to obtain a confession and could even be killed for the general good of Christianity: a different tradition – one which called for love of sinner without accepting the sin[6] – remained alive in the tradition and in preaching, but never became mandatory in the Latin church.[7] In the discipline of the late Middle Ages and modern times, we can therefore see a strengthening of the institutions of the Inquisition in the Roman Church. Here the anonymous bureaucracy of the procedures seemed to guarantee something more than the zeal of indiviuals: in this way a true 'Holy Office' came into being with a 'universal' jusrsdiction and a 'supreme' authority.[8] In connection with the development of private penitence it was charged with disciplining the consciences and punishing the bodies of those who dared to refuse to *sentire cum ecclesia*, to accept the mind of the church.[9]

From the perspective of this punitive doctrine, those who got involved with such organs and were put to death at the end of a process which was often formally scrupulous were not in fact martyrs (unless, as in the case of Hus, the view was taken that the church was being punished in its founder or representative); the martyr is as such *in odium fidei*, so the rebel in the faith can make his victims martyrs, but cannot be other than a criminal, guilty of *lèse majesté* against God. The one who is injured by the heretic is God, whose honour is rescued by the confession and then by the killing of the guilty party;[10] the soul of the criminal, too, is lost as a result of the sin of heresy but the proceedings, through confession or torture, bring about what is necessary to redeem it. This is the argument of the theory of the Inquisition in modern times. And thanks to these principles the ecclesiastical authorities act in two capacities: they consign the condemned person to the secular arm for execution since the clergy, an estate in Christianity distinct from the laity, are forbidden to shed blood, but by doing this the church is again, *in extremis*, taking upon itself the cure of the soul of the condemned person. In fact both the most 'famous' victims of religious repression (from Girolamo Savonarola to Giordano Bruno) and the anonymous ranks of those killed in the struggle against heresy and Protestantism were interrogated and judged by ecclesiastical organs, but in the end were handed over to the political power for punishment. Thus after taking responsibility for the condemnation, the religious figures – often in the form of the friar who accompanied the condemned person to the stake – reappeared in a neutral position alongside the victim, to whom they offered spiritual comforts which did not cancel out the crime but pardoned the sin.[11] In some cases – we need think only of Joan of Arc – the church could also return to a process in order to revise documents and judgments, but only if this did not put the conduct of the ecclesiastical authority of the time in question. In any case, until after Vatican II, when a condemation was individual, capital and canonical, there was no possibility of appeal or acknowledgment of error.

The case of those who were condemned in the great disputes between theological schools is different. The dispute on poverty, the disagreement over the right of the mendicants to preach, the struggle against Jansenism, the conflict between maculists and immaculists, the polemic on quietism, the battle for or against the Society of Jesus, the division over the infallibility and the primacy of the pope, certainly produced victimizations caused by the church itself. However, these were on a level which recognized the possibility of revisions of positions which were not final, at least until dogmatization intervened to settle the question and to call for absolute submission, as happened in various circumstances up to 1956.[12]

II. Continuity and new developments in the twentieth century

Some of these experiences and mentalities of condemnation continued well into the twentieth century; but there were also new elements. There was an end to the regime of the temporal power of Christendom, and the image of the enemy of the church also changed colour:[13] he was no longer the herald of another truth resistant to any change of heart, but a traitor, manifest or hidden; knowingly or unknowingly he enjoyed the favour of the great global adversary, modernity.

In the eyes of Pope Pius X, the many great ferments in society and culture at the dawn of the new century, often welcomed by men of letters, philosophers and Catholic theologians as the occasion for a 'new apologetic', become one great enemy, denounced in the encyclical *Pascendi* of 8 September 1907 and pursued until the outbreak of the first World War and beyond. With the hunt for those guilty of modernism – according to Pius X 'the synthesis of all heresies' – the system of condemnations made a qualitative leap:[14] the 'guilty' were identified on the basis of denunciations and charges made through private channels; the church condemned and excommunicated both those who had been convinced of their own positions and those to whom the stubbornness of their accusers left no escape. However, hundreds of theologians and clergy professed their innocence unheard and in the end decided to submit to their condemnation (*laudabiliter se subjecit* is the note in their files), not in order to escape physical punishment but out of a supernatural obedience towards an injustice on the part of the authorities. In this way a sort of surreptitious penalty was introduced which the condemned person inflicted on himself. This was a punishment which in some cases also punished the bishops: not only did they become objects of suspicion,[15] but they had to communicate to their clergy provisions made by Rome which went against their own wills and consciences, while at the time maintaining secrecy (*reticito nomine*) about who was truly behind the action. They had to bear the moral burden of this action. Despite the fact that so many people resigned themselves to injustice out of 'love for the church', the moral, spirtual and theological harm done here was incalculable.[16] A Europe which had lacked a theological vigilance that kept up with the times became mired in the mud of war and totalitarianism; and the victims of this campaign, which was extended throughout the first half of the twentieth century by secret societies and the teaching of the church, were not to receive any reparations until the beginning of Vatican II, when historians turned to examine the phenomenon of modernism and its repression.[17]

In 1942, the symbolic placing on the Index of Prohibited Books in 1942 of a lecture by Fr Marie-Dominique Chenu on theological method given by the learned Dominican at the beginning of a course at Le Saulchoir six years previously indicated that this anti-modernism would remain as a paradigm in the new season of condemnations which can be said to have opened then.[18] Unlike the repression of Action Française, which involved marked political elements,[19] or the condemnation of ecumenism in 1928, in which some pioneers succeeded in explaining the reason for their actions,[20] the decision to punish the Dominican teacher and his view of the relationship between history and theology indicated the dominance in Rome of a renewed culture of suspicion directed against theological research, though moves were now made with greater formality by comparison with the years of Pius X, when an arrogant attitude was not afraid to take short cuts. Many would feel the weight of this development in the years to come: the Jesuits of Lyons who began the patristic collection Sources Chrétiennes;[21] the philosophers alienated by the contant repetition of neo-Thomism in teaching;[22] the exponents of what was to be called *la nouvelle théologie*;[23] the innovators involved in pastoral work and the mission of the worker-priests;[24] all those Catholics who had fallen under suspicion after the excommunication of the Communists in 1949 which (without bothering the parties of the Third International) deepened the gulf betwen the church and the working class in the West.[25] Hit first by specific measures implemented by the religious orders to which they belonged, the theologians of this generation became the subject of a whole encyclical – *Humani generis* of 12 August 1950 – in which Pius XII repudiated the attempt that they had made to produce an understanding of the faith which was adequate to the challenge of modern times and the post-war period.

The studies which now describe the steps in this new stage of persecution, culminating with the beatification of Pope Sarto,[26] paint a broad and depressing picture, created by those who believed that they had a duty to serve the church with their intellectual rigour and their severe censors who felt it their duty to put a stop to this with every means possible. We now have the diary of one of the greatest theologians of this generation, Fr Yves-Marie Congar, later to be made a cardinal. Congar gives an account of the years of persecution which he endured with despair and indomitable dignity with the aim of advancing the cause of ecumenism in the church.[27] The diary does not explain why Congar 'remained'[28] (leaving was a freedom which was not allowed before Vatican II): it relates with a rare dramatic intensity the arrogance of an ecclesiastical power which sets no limits to itself, and the perplexity of a believer driven to the edge of suicide by charges which never took account of his own consistency, forced to a silence which stripped him of any capacity to exercise his apostolate – the term which Congar then preferred – which was at one with his vocation and his identity.[29]

A churchman of the rank of the Substitute for the Secretary of State, Mgr Montini, was a victim in this period. When the future Paul VI spoke of the need not only to suffer for the cause of the church he was also alluding to himself: granted, he had not suffered penalties, but he had been driven out of Rome in 1953 with a classic 'promotion to get rid of him'. This was devised by a collection of ecclesiastics who, putting pressure on the pope,

Suffering Because of the Church

succeeded in having Montini designated Archbishop of Milan and then omitted to make him a cardinal, a step which would have made him a natural candidate to succeed Pacelli. No accusations of a doctrinal kind were made against Montini – who had simply stated that 'prudence is no longer enough; there is a need for prudence to become astuteness'.[30] However, his intellectual curiosity and his sensitivity to the problematical authorities of the theological culture – qualities which in any case seemed to be unacceptably opposed to a repressive system which necessarily struck without regard for persons and without reflecting on reasons – were important factors for the secret conspiracy which moved him from the Vatican.[31]

III. The period of the Council

The season of condemnations experienced a moment of painful and profound rethinking at Vatican II. This process was begun by the decision of John XXIII not to use condemnations in conciliar decisions, a decision spelt out in his speech at the opening of Vatican II; it was endorsed by the work of the bishops in the course of the debates and then extended in the period after the Council, ending in the 'revision' of the trial of Galileo, the *Tertio millennio adveniente* of John Paul II and the *mea culpa* of the Second Sunday in Lent of the Jubilee of 2000. These are elements of a broader story, parts of which have already been reconstructed elsewhere.[32] However, we need to recall some elements here.

1. It is in fact well known that from its very preparation Vatican II was polarized. On the one hand Pope John indicated with great clarity that the Council was not to threaten new condemnations because it was meant to be an act of discerning the signs of the times, rather than imposing sanctions on errors.[33] On the other hand the Roman Curia, which had been entrusted with the internal preparation of the ecumenical council, was composed of individuals who by culture and experience had lived within the condemnations as a form of governance.[34] In the middle were the few theologians who, having been persecuted in the previous years, found themselves involved so to speak as hostages in the preparatory phase, in the expectation that the event of the Coucil itself would shuffle the cards,[35] and who wanted to see whether Vatican II really signified a more than superficial renewal of ways of thinking.

2. Just as the Council was about to meet, in the summer of 1962, what was to happen began to become clear: the very moment the first schemata were circulated, a new relationship began between bishops and theologians which

gave legitimation to almost a whole generation which had previously been under suspicion.[36] The bishops needed lessons in theology so that they could join in the great doctrinal, institutional and spiritual issues which the occasion of the Council required; and the theologians needed the episcopate, as supremely represented at the Council in the sight of all the churches present along with their observers, to indicate a recognition that freedom of research was useful and necessary for the church and to guarantee that it was physiologically grafted on to the body of the church. The speech with which John XXIII opened the Council on 11 October 1962 was also governed by this demand: in distancing himself from the 'prophets of doom' the pope stated that their error and the reason for their gloom was their belief that the world had existed 'for half a century', i.e. only from the modernist crisis onwards. He asserted that the Council must not just repeat dogmas but allow 'a leap forward' in the understanding of the mystery of Christ. This ruled out condemnations as an instrument.[37]

3. A departure from the logic of the condemnations did not entail a call for compensation for a professional group which had certainly been unjustly disadvantaged; it raised a specifically institutional question. This became evident in the debates in the Council: a famous speech given by Cardinal Frings on 8 November 1963 bears symbolic testimony to their high quality.[38] During the discussion of the relationship between the Curia and the bishops, the Archbishop of Cologne asked for a distinction to be made between the methods of administration and the methods of jurisdiction in all the Roman dicasteries, including the Holy Office, 'whose procedure is in many respects no longer in keeping with our age, is harmful to the church and an object of scandal to many'. Though it could be understood to refer to recent events,[39] his demand that 'no one should be condemned before being heard and having had the possibility of correcting himself' was meant generally: Frings was not asking for a code of procedure but for a reform of the conception of authority. This was understood by Cardinal Ottaviani, who could claim the modest but real merit of having reduced capricious elements dating from the time of Pius X.[40] He fulminated against those who 'out of ignorance, not to say worse' had criticized 'the Supreme Congregation of the Holy Office, its President and the Summus Pontifex'. It was also understood by the bishops who applauded Frings, thus revealing how deeply the problem denounced by the German cardinal and then by others was felt everywhere – over and above any personal cases.[41]

However, the question of the institutional architecture of the central government was left open:[42] Vatican II could not deal with it, although Paul

Suffering Because of the Church

VI wanted to honour the pledge made to the Curia that the reform of this body should not move into the aula of the synod – and that was how it was to be. But the climate of the Council and the period after the Council confirmed the perception that the season of condemnations was now over. The idea of making Congar a cardinal (this was being talked of in 1965) and abolishing the Index of Prohibited Books were so to speak a signal that the Church of Rome was turning the page and leaving behind the pernicious climate denounced by Cardinal Montini ten years previously. Bascially, even the malicious gossip of the traditionalists who accused Pope John XXIII of being a modernist[43] recognized that the 'step forward' had been taken with Vatican II and that Catholicism wanted to keep all the dialectic within the church as a dynamism to be welcomed without naivety, and without untimely dramatizations.

IV. After Vatican II

The reform of the Roman Curia in 1967, announced by Paul VI in his role as 'chief reformer' of Catholicism, largely took account of this climate. While continuing to retain the political and institutional body which at the end of the 1950s was thought to be an indispensable instrument of the new post-war and post-conciliar papacy, Paul VI redistributed responsibilities, put a priority on decision-making, reorganized posts, and revised and retouched the reforms introduced sixty years previously by Pius X. The Secretary of State became head of the Vatican executive, while the old Holy Office lost its sinister name and eloquent adjective ('supreme'), which had been shorthand indicating those places whose acts and norms remained secret.[44] However, the course of events after the Council in the 1970s split off some of the proposed reforms, which the Apostolic Constitution *Regimini Ecclesiae* sought to interpret: despite the appointment of Cardinal Seper as head of the new Congregation for the Doctrine of Faith, which was meant to change the climate and style of Ottaviani's way of doing things, the very idea of Paul VI that he could or should direct the post-conciliar period from Rome, personally taking charge as bridge-builder between the conflicting parties and providing solutions, exacerbated the already bitter conflicts between the church authorities and the theologians, whether on points which remained open after Vatican II (from collegial structures to hormonal contraception) or those which the reception of the Council forced on the attention of the church (from poverty to communion).

Over and above the names, the adjectives, and finally the intentions, what happened was that the Roman centre returned to the centre of the conflict. The theologians found themselves faced with an organ which in itself represented a conception of the truth as propositions and on this basis read fragments of text with a total disregard for the concern to make a distinctive voice heard.[45] Bishops, too, felt the unease caused by the withdrawal of Rome's trust: some were deposed in circumstances which, however complex, had an air of oppression: the removal of Cardinal Lercaro from the see of Bologna, the substitution of Mgr Baldassari at Ravenna, the move of Pellegrino to Turin – to mention just Italy – and then the process over the Bishop of Guernavaca, Dom Sergio Mendez Arceo, are only some of the more striking cases of the way in which 'suffering because of the church' did not end with the season of condemnations.[46] Other bishops in the countries of Eastern Europe, misled by the disinformation disseminated by the Communist regimes, felt that the open dialogue in *Ostpolitik* was a way of trampling over them as a punishment; the bishops of some episcopal conferences – from the Netherlands to Brazil, and from Peru to the United States – suffered under episcopal nominations aimed at breaking down the majority and shifting the political balance in the collegial organs.[47] In other words, the failures to understand after the Council were just as wide-ranging as the failures to understand before it.

Actual 'cases' developed over and against theologians: three elements – the climate of counter-information which attracted the febrile interest of public opinion, the legitimation of 'dissidence' in the political sphere which was being emphasized at that time, and the weight of the new generation of clergy trained during Vatican II – contributed towards upsetting the way in which suffering because of the church had been spiritualized. The secrecy which had prevailed in earlier cases was broken and the arguments of both the prosecution and the defence were presented on the media. first against Edward Schillebeeckx and then against Hans Küng, some of those proceedings began which were to have greater weight in delineating the 'political doctrine' of the new Congregation for the Doctrine of the Faith: the conflict was not just about specialists, but flared up over works addressed to a broad public, or on topics which were widely controversial in the practice of Christians and Christian communities. Alongside these 'cases', more local proceedings multiplied, bound up with the rivalry within Catholic faculties, in which the authority of Rome allowed itself to become involved. In one case after another, the provisions made by Rome, far from preventing the spread of ideas or interrupting the discussion of individual issues, punished individual scholars unseen to colleagues or fellow religious, along with their bishops, who could only very rarely be considered to be the initiators of such controversies.

The media, in a way typical of the press at the end of the twentieth century, created new dynamics: the victims of the repression often found themselves in the limelight of notoriety and, whether they liked it or not, assumed the role of symbols instead of being able to develop their own intellectual and theological careers; the Roman organs found themselves responding to the actions of secondary figures and exposed to public scorn when they should have been explaining the criteria and methods which were invisible to the majority of public opinion; and finally the papacy found itself led into making some of the most famous victims of the system of condemnations cardinals when they reached the age of eighty as an act of public reparation.[48]

Dealing with this institutional, doctrinal, procedural and media-driven tangle was entrusted by John Paul II in 1981 to a professional theologian who had been *peritus* to Cardinal Frings at Vatican II. Joseph Ratzinger was appointed prefect of the Congregation for the Doctrine of Faith after brief diocesan experience; this appointment was also meant to counter the feeling that the examination of doctrine was being carried out by individuals whose academic qualifications were not high.[49] As in the 1967 reform, the proposals were overtaken by reality: the Congregation – though wanting to use a more transparent procedure – has not ceased to take steps to censor theologians over views thought to be erroneous, but the awareness of theologians has now changed. As has been evident in the bitter fight against liberation theology, which used the Marxist analysis of capitalism,[50] and against representatives of other theological disciplines (Curran, or Drewermann, and now Tillard), the Congregation used the process as a punishment. The result was that neither those who were willing to retract nor those who were not recognized the right of that organ to put their conscience in question.

So in the last decade the signs of a change of course have been increasing: alongside the proceedings against individuals, sometimes anticipated or replaced by direct attacks by the Cardinal Prefect in lectures which he gives as a 'private' theologian, the Congregation, by itself and through the papal magisterium, has worked in three directions: first, it has constructed images of doctrine (*Donum veritatis*), theological criteria (*Veritatis splendor*) and canonical procedures (*Ad tuendam fidem*) which are to be taken as universally valid; secondly, it has produced a series of instructions on topical questions, trying to overturn ecumenical (*Ordinatio sacerdotalis*), theological (*Dominus Iesus*) or liturgical debates which are far from being over; finally, it has subjected to examination individual authors whom, while praising their intentions, it has stigmatized as 'ambiguous'. Precisely because they are given this epithet their supposed errors are not easy to recognize objectively and they have no way of escaping the shadows of suspicion (as has been seen in the recent cases of Dupuis, Messner and Vidal).[51] The accumulation of instructions, notes, *motu proprios* and condemnations makes the area of possible 'ambiguity' even greater and increases the risk of victimizations which are difficult to deal with.

V. Barren suffering?

So has the suffering which Cardinal Montini denounced in the middle of the last century as an inevitable and anxious condition of some Catholics come to an end? Has it been reabsorbed by the troubles endured by those theologians who are thought to be 'ambiguous', the targets of actions which do not satisfy the basic principles of canon law? Will no one now savour the spiritual bitterness of those who – from Oscar Romero to Ignacio Ellacuría – have felt in their very deaths the effect of an unjust abandonment and isolation? Does the image of the prefect of the Congregation for the Doctrine of Faith who in Lent of the great Jubilee Year mounted the pulpit in St Peter's to ask pardon from God for the crimes committed by the church in the name of the church guarantee that the useless suffering caused by an idea of the truth which has no pity will no longer be tolerated?[52]

Perhaps not: not so much because there will be those who (like the women who had themselves 'ordained' in 2002) are ready to trade condemnation for visibility;[53] nor because the method of denunciation currently used allows envy to create new cases where the church has nothing to fear and where the bishops can quietly see to things by themselves. In the end all this could be attributed to a physiological margin of error in a great institution or to a period which has still to digest Vatican II completely. A certain useless, unacceptable suffering will continue for those ordinary believers who have almost no awareness of the way in which the magisterium is continually taking positions – from the very general ones on ordination, catechisms, the encounter between Christianity and other faiths, relations between sister churches, divorce and the role of the laity to the homily and confession – but cannot help feeling that the more profoundly human issues (the desire for life, the need for forgiveness, the quest for communion, personal relations) have no place in the church. This is a suffering which after Vatican II can no longer be accepted as the 'quasi-martyrdom' of a dolorist institutional spirituality. Certainly it can scandalize, or it can be experienced with

Suffering Because of the Church 117

disenchanted patience within the faith, in a church which in this way is learning a confession that is incompatible with the gospel and always feels the injustice produced within it as a thorn in the flesh which prevents any feelings of pride.

Translated by John Bowden

Notes

1. As attested by D. M. Turoldo, *La mia vita per gli amici*, ed M. Nicolai Paynter, Milan 2001, p. 121.
2. Cf. A. Riccardi, *Il potere del papa da Pio XII a Giovanni Paolo II*, Roma and Bari 1993, pp. 142–48.
3. É. Fouilloux, *Une église en quête de liberté: la pensée catholique française entre modernisme et Vatican II*, Paris 1998, and *Au coeur du XXe siècle religieux*, Paris 1993.
4. W. Doskocil, *Der Bann in der Urkirche. Eine rechtsgeschichtliche Untersuchung*, Munich 1958, and K. Hein, *Eucharist and Excommunication. A Study in Early Christian Doctrine and Discipline*, Frankfurt am Main 1975. Cf. also N. McLynn, 'Christian Controversy and Violence in the Fourth Century', *Kodai* 1992/3, pp. 15–44.
5. E. Vodola, *Excommunication in the Middle Ages*, Berkeley 1986, and R. Maceratini, *Ricerche sullo status giuridico dell'eretico nel diritto romano-cristiano e nel diritto canonico classico (da Graziano a Uguccione)*, Padua 1994.
6. P. Brown, 'St Augustine's Attitude to Religious Coercion', *Journal of Roman Studies* 54, 1964, pp. 107–16.
7. D. Baker (ed), *Schism, Heresy and Protest*, Cambridge 1972, and W. J. Sheils (ed), *Persecution and Toleration*, Studies in Church History 21, Oxford 1984.
8. E. Brambilla, *Alle origini del Sant'Uffizio. Penitenza, confessione e giustizia spirituale dal medioevo al XVI secolo*, Bologna 2000.
9. A. Prosperi, *I tribunali della coscienza. Inquisitori, confessori, missionari*, Turin 1996.
10. M. Sbriccoli, *Crimen laese majestatis. Il problema del reato politico alle soglie della scienza penalistica moderna*, Milan 1974.
11. Scott L. Waugh and Peter D. Diehl (eds), *Christendom and Its Discontents: Exclusion, Persecution and Rebellion 1000–1500*, Cambridge 1996, and P. Prodi, *Una storia della giustizia. Dal pluralismo dei fori al moderno dualismo tra coscienza e diritto*, Bologna 2000.
12. Cf. H-J. Pottmeyer, 'Lo sviluppo della teologia dell'ufficio papale nel contesto ecclesiologico, sociale ed ecumenico del XX secolo', in *Chiesa e papato nel XX secolo*, ed G. Alberigo and A. Riccardi, Bari 1990, pp. 3–63.
13. Cf. G. Ruggieri (ed), *I nemici della cristianità*, Bologna 1997.

14. P. Colin, *L'audace et le soupçon: la crise dans le catholicisme français 1893–1914*, Paris 1997.
15. This was the case, for example, with the Bishop of Bergamo between 1904 and 1914, whose secretary was Angelo G. Roncalli, the future pope. In his biography, Roncalli wrote that the bishop, 'particularly in these last years, was torn with uncertainty and doubt as to whether he any longer enjoyed the trust of the Holy Father. This was the greatest proof of his virtue, and though today it could be a very delicate matter to speak about, to keep silent about it could be a grave breach of the truth and a lack of fairness to the real merits of Msgr Radini.' A. G. Roncalli, *Mons. Giacomo Radini Tedeschi, vescovo di Bergamo*, Bergamo 1913 (^{3}1963).
16. This was a problem raised in December 1949 by the *Romana beatificationis et canonizationis Servi Dei Pii Papæ X – Disquisitio circa quasdam obiectiones modum agendi Servi Dei [scil. Pii X] respicientes in modernismi debelleatione una cum summario additionali ex officio compilato*, Typis Polyglottis Vaticanis 1950, pp. iv–vi. Here it was asked whether in this phase the pope had shown some lack of prudence 'or of love and justice'; for the whole of the pontificate; cf. *Pio X*, ed G. La Bella.
17. Cf. E. Poulat, *Intégrisme et catholicisme intégral. Un réseau secret international antimoderniste: La Sapinère (1909–1921)*, Tournai 1969, and now also G. Vian, *La riforma della chiesa per la restaurazione cristiana della società* (2 vols), Rome 1998.
18. M.-D. Chenu, *Une école de théologie: le Saulchoir, 1937*, Paris 1985, with articles by G. Alberigo and É. Fouilloux (French version of the first Italian edition, Casale Monferrato 1982); also A. Riccardi, 'Una "école de théologie" fra la Francia e Roma', *Cristianesimo nella storia* 5, 1984, pp. 11–28.
19. J. Prevotat, *Les Catholiques et l'Action française. Histoire d'une condamnation. 1899–1939*, Paris 2001.
20. Cf. É. Fouilloux, *Les catholiques et l'unité chrétiénne du XIXe au XXe siècle. Itinéraires européennes d'expression française*, Paris 1982. For the career and the figure of the founder of the monastery of Chevetogne, cf. *Veiller avant l'aurore. Colloque Beauduin*, Chevetogne, and R. Loonbeek and J. Mortiau, *Un pionnier, dom Lambert Beauduin (1873–1960). Liturgie et Unité des chrètiens*, Louvain-la-Neuve 2001.
21. É. Fouilloux, *La collection 'Sources Chrétiennes'. Éditer les Pères de l'Église au XXe siècle*, Paris 1995.
22. For the generation of the 1920s see P. Chenaux, *Entre Maurras et Maritain – Une génération intellectuelle catholique (1920–1930)*, Paris 1999.
23. Cf. Fouilloux, *Une église en quête de liberté* (n.3). He also provides the best bibliography on the topic.
24. F. Leprieur, *Quand Rome condamne. Dominicains et prêtres-ouvriers*, Paris 1989.
25. G. Alberigo, 'La condanna della collaborazione dei cattolici con i partiti

Suffering Because of the Church 119

comunisti', *Concilium* 1975, 7, pp. 145–58, and Riccardi, *Il potere del papa* (n.2), pp. 88–99.

26. A. Riccardi, 'Pio X, santo di Pio XII', in *Pio X. Un papa e il suo tempo*, ed. G. Romanato, Cinisello Balsamo 1987, pp. 237–41.
27. J. Fameree, *Histoire et Eglise. L'ecclésiologie du père Congar de 'Chrétiens désunis' à l'annonce du Concile (1937–1959)*, Louvain-la-Neuve 1991.
28. Cf. H. Urs von Balthasar and J. Ratzinger, *Perché sono ancora cristiano – Perché sono ancora nella chiesa*, Brescia 1972.
29. Y. Congar, *Journal d'un théologien 1946–1956*, with an introduction and edited by É. Fouilloux, Paris 2000.
30. Cf. O. Fallaci, *Vita del prete Lorenzo Milani*, Milan 1974, p. 247.
31. Cf. A. Riccardi, *Il 'partito romano' nel secondo dopoguerra*, Brescia 1983.
32. Alberto Melloni (ed), *Storia del concilio Vaticano II diretta da Giuseppe Alberigo* (5 vols), Bologna 1995–2001.
33. Cf. G. Alberigo, 'L'annuncio del concilio', in *Storia del concilio Vaticano II* 1, pp. 50–60.
34. Cf. G. Alberigo and A. Melloni (eds), *Verso il concilio Vaticano II (1960–1962)*, Genoa 1993, and G. Alberigo (ed), *Il Vaticano II fra attese e celebrazione*, Bologna 1995.
35. Cf. É. Fouilloux, 'Comment devient-on expert à Vatican II? Le cas du père Yves Congar', in *Le deuxième concile du Vatican (1959–1965)*, Rome 1989, pp. 307–31.
36. With some exceptions, like Chenu, cf. his testimony in M.-D. Chenu, *Notes quotidiennes au Concile*, Paris 1995.
37. For the text, of which there is a very important autograph manuscript, cf. G. Alberigo and A. Melloni, 'L'allocuzione Gaudet Mater Ecclesia (11 ottobre 1962)', in *Fede Tradizione Profezia. Studi su Giovanni XXIII e sul Vaticano II*, Brescia 1984, 210–83.
38. Cf. *Acta Synodalia*, Rome 1966, pars II, vol. 4, pp. 616–18.
39. The withdrawal from the bookshops in Rome of H. Küng, *The Council and Reunion* (original German edition Freiburg im Breisgau 1963, Italian edition Turin 1964) at the opening of the second period of the Council is certainly not unconnected with this passage in Frings' speech.
40. For Ottaviani cf. E. Cavaterra, *Il prefetto del Sant'Offizio*, Milan 1990.
41. Cf. the memoirs of J. Frings, *Für die Menschen bestellt. Erinnerungen*, Cologne 1973, 274. On 1 October 1965 the newly-elected Archbishop of Turin, Michele Pellegrino, denounced in the aula the Congar case, of which he had direct knowledge; for the Dominican's reaction cf. *Mon Journal du Concile*, an edition of the typescript of which is announced, edited by the French province.
42. For the material withdrawn cf. *Storia del Vaticano II*, index.
43. The accusation, which was circulated in traditionalist circles after the Council, had been made in November 1962 by the *Corriere della sera* with a series of

articles signed by I. Montanelli, who had reported the content of conversations with Cardinal Palazzini, cf. G. Zizola, *Giovanni XXIII, la fede e la politica*, Rome and Bari 2000, p. 207.

44. For the *motu proprio Integræ servandæ* on the restructuring of the Sacred Congregation for the Doctrine of Faith, dated 7 December 1965, *AAS* 57, 1965, pp. 952–55, cf. Riccardi, *Il potere del papa da Pio XII a Giovanni Paolo II* (n.2), pp. 289–300.
45. Cf. G. Ruggieri, 'La politica dottrinale della curia romana nel postconcilio', *Cristianesimo nella storia* 21, 2000, pp. 103–31.
46. For Lercaro cf. G.Dossetti, 'Memoria di Giacomo Lercaro', in *Chiese italiane e concilio. Esperienze pastorali nella chiesa italiana da Pio XII a Paolo VI*, ed G. Alberigo, Genoa 1988, pp. 281–312.
47. For the Brazilian and Dutch conferences see the studies by J. O. Beozzo and A. Y. H. A. Jacobs.
48. Paul VI and John Paul II have given this honour, though without the right to vote in the conclave, to distinguished theologians like H. De Lubac, H.U. von Balthasar, A. Grillmeier, Y. Congar and other figures less well known to the wider public, like P. Pavan, Rector of the Lateran, who drafted *Pacem in terris*, and Roberto Tucci, editor of *Civiltà Cattolica*.
49. The appointment was made on 25 November 1981; for the relationship between the former professor of moral theology in Lublin and the famous Regensburg fundamental theologian, the testimony of the latter is important: J. Ratzinger, *Giovanni Paolo II. Vent'anni nella storia*, Cinisello Balsamo 1999; for the previous phase cf. *La mia vita. Ricordi (1927–1977)*, Cinisello Balsamo 1997.
50. The ideology of repression (which in some circles has been structured as a 'theology of liberation from communism' through violence) has been progressively disowned by the Holy See and the episcopates, though there have been many problems. For its significance in the case of Argentina cf. J. Klaiber, *The Church, Dictatorships, and Democracy in Latin America*, 1998.
51. Cf. My 'Recent Notifications on the Works of Reinhard Messner, Jacques Dupuis and Marciano Vidal', *Concilium* 2002/5.
52. The text on the site www.vatican.va, in the section news_services/liturgy/documents, was printed in *Osservatore Romano* on 12 March 2000: 'We pray that each one of us, recognizing that men of the church, too, in the name of faith and morality, have sometimes had recourse to methods which are not in keeping with the gospel in the conviction that they had to defend the faith, will know how to imitate our Lord Jesus, who was gentle and humble of heart.'
53. For the seven women priests and the excommunication which has been sought and gained see the chronicles by John Allen in the *National Catholic Reporter*.

IV. The Struggle and Hope that Make Martyrs

The Crucified People as 'Light for the Nations': A Reflection on Ignacio Ellacuría

KEVIN F. BURKE

Introduction: A biblical formula?

The formula framed by the title of this essay does not appear on the pages of scripture. However, it contains rich allusions to the Old Testament and echoes the counter-intuitive logic of numerous gospel sayings. *The last shall be first. Blessed are you who are poor. Whatever you did for one of my least brothers or sisters, you did for me. Whoever loses his or her life for the gospel will save it.*[1] More importantly, it locates the gospel as a whole where it belongs: in history and among the victims of history. In fact, the theological potency of this formula springs from the evangelical poignancy with which it names the victims.

The dramatic and quasi-scandalous image, 'crucified people', unites the marred faces of the world's victims with the battered countenance of the suffering messiah. Coined by Ignacio Ellacuría, it denotes a historical reality that functions as a crucial sign of our times. Rooted in the *Spiritual Exercises* of St Ignatius Loyola, it frames a composition of place for contemporary followers of Jesus. Applied to salvation theory, it carries forward the concrete implications of the saving action of Jesus *qua* servant whom God establishes as 'light for the nations' (Isa. 42.6). These three images – the crucified people as *sign*, as *place*, and as *servant* – give content to the overarching messianic metaphor, *light for the nations*. I submit that, by drawing on this formula, believers may encounter anew the ancient mystery of martyrdom and rediscover the access it provides to a saving encounter with the crucified Lord. Following Ellacuría's intuitions, I respond to the invitation to 'rethink martyrdom' with an essay in historical soteriology,[2] accenting the way Christians encounter, respond to, and correspond with God's gift of salvation here and now. Thus, I do not focus on martyrdom *per se*, but on that to which martyrdom witnesses: salvation as *salvation in history*.

I. Sign of the times

In several key texts, the Second Vatican Council directs the church's attention to the signs of the times and the evangelical requirement prayerfully to read and discern them. In the light of this powerful mandate, Ellacuría comments:

> Among so many signs always being given, some identified and others hardly perceptible, there is in every age one that is primary, in whose light we should discern and interpret all the rest. This perennial sign is the historically crucified people, who link their permanence to ever distinct forms of their crucifixion. This crucified people represents the historical continuation of the servant of Yahweh, who is forever being stripped of his human features by the sin of the world, who is forever being despoiled of everything by the powerful of this world, who is forever being robbed even of life, especially of life.[3]

Prior to its function as a sign of the times, the crucified people is a historical reality.[4] But the phrase, 'crucified people', does not refer to the sum total of all individual injuries and griefs. Rather, it identifies the vast but specific class of persons who live each day in the shadow of death, their most basic human needs perpetually unsatisfied. It encompasses those who languish without adequate education, health care, work, or the means to change their lot. In our world these people represent the overwhelming majority. Some forty million of their children die of hunger every year. Yet they have no voice. They do not count. With terrible pathos Jon Sobrino notes that, as a consequence of our present world order, 'a "subspecies" of the nonexistent, the superfluous, the excluded has made its appearance'.[5]

Apologists for the present world order deem its inequities regrettable but unavoidable. They cannot directly deny the extent or severity of historical *suffering*. However, they can try to distance themselves from that suffering by denying responsibility for it, above all, by interpreting it as anything but *historical* suffering. So they construct a-historical versions of the 'real world' to mask the historical connections between wealth and poverty, power and violence, access and marginalization. But the language of crucified people directly challenges all of this. It unmasks the present world order by reconnecting the appearance of the 'subspecies of the nonexistent' with the parallel appearance of obscene wealth and narrow concentrations of power. These realities do not result from fate or evolutionary determinism. Excessive wealth and poverty are among the direct, dialectically related consequences of multiple human decisions, actions, omissions, traditions, and structures. The inhuman poverty suffered by the people is not a 'tragedy'. It is a consequence of human freedom and represents historical mortal sin. Ellacuría emphasizes the structural character of this historical sin when he describes the crucified people as 'that collective body which, as the majority of humankind, owes its situation of crucifixion to the way society is organized and maintained by a minority that exercises its dominion through a series of factors, which taken together and given their concrete impact within history, must be regarded as sin'.[6]

Analysing global systems in terms of historical sin is politically dangerous. It involves naming individual and corporate crucifiers, and undraping the mechanisms of torture and execution hidden in mundane realities like structural adjustment programmes, free trade zones, national security measures, and wars on terrorism. It leads to direct confrontations with idolatrous powers, powers that retaliate when challenged, as Ellacuría's own fate testifies. Thus, the potent phrase, 'crucified people', demands an accounting from those who profit from crucifixion and, in a different way, from those who follow Christ. Here, then, we have an initial way in which the crucified people functions as light for the nations: it unmasks the world's sin and exposes its need for conversion, redemption, and renewal.

II. Revelatory place

In the process of identifying the truth of the world, the crucified people points to where Christians encounter God in history. Accordingly, there appears a second level of its constitution as light for the nations that corresponds to the spiritual roots of Ellacuría's theology. Not only does the crucified people point (as sign) to a historical reality; it embodies a *locus* where the human and divine intersect, an exemplary *revelatory place*.[7] It manifests where, in our world today, the authentic mystical-political encounter with the crucified and risen Christ occurs.

Ellacuría did not accidentally stumble on the phrase, 'crucified people'. Familiarity with the *Spiritual Exercises* of St Ignatius Loyola led him to it. In a striking meditation that appears near the end of the first Week of the *Exercises*, St Ignatius instructs the believer to kneel before the crucified and ask, 'What have I done for Christ? What am I doing for Christ? What ought I to do for Christ?'[8] In an article written from El Salvador to the churches of his native Spain, Ellacuría alludes to this well-known colloquy. He urges his readers to open their hearts to those suffering from misery, hunger, oppression, and repression, and 'before this people thus crucified' to ask, 'What have I done to crucify them? What am I doing to end their crucifixion? What should I do so that this people might rise from the dead?'[9]

There is more at work here than the arbitrary association of a historical reality with a religious symbol of salvific suffering. A key element in Ellacuría's theological method involves what he calls 'historicization', the operation by which he seeks to understand *theological* concepts as part of an ongoing, transformative *historical* process. To historicize a theological concept means to grasp how its usage interacts with a particular historical reality, impelling believers to take responsibility for the ongoing conversion of that reality. This operation, which Ellacuría develops philosophically at great length, corresponds to a foundational moment in the Ignatian *Exercises*. Repeatedly Ignatius urges the one making the *Exercises* to begin a period of prayer with a 'composition of place'. By means of this composition, one is situated in the 'history' of salvation. Similarly, Ellacuría says that the *Exercises* 'historicize the word of God insofar as they turn to historical, personal and situational signs so that that word might be discovered in the concrete'. More importantly, they 'make the historical into the essential part of the structure of the Christian encounter with God'.[10]

As we saw above, Ellacuría's language of the crucified people illuminates a historical reality. Here we notice that it does something more. It historicizes a revelatory reality, the ongoing presence in history of Jesus Christ. The Christian community finds the crucified Jesus in the crucified people, and it follows the messianic Jesus when it labours to take that people down from the cross. This historicization of the Christian vision enables the church to recover its fundamental identity as the community of the risen Lord's disciples. Likewise, it impels the church to fulfill its mission by proclaiming anew the central Gospel paradox: in the very place of death God is revealed as the God of life.[11]

III. Servant of Yahweh

To call the victims of our world 'crucified people' both confronts a scandalous historical reality and reveals the pre-eminent place for finding God in our world. Now a third dimension of the crucified people as light for the nations dawns. Ellacuría observes that 'what Christian faith adds to the historical verification of the oppressed people is the suspicion that, besides being the principle addressee of the work of salvation, it might also be, in its very crucified situation, a principle of salvation for the whole world'.[12] To illustrate how this could be he probes the logic of suffering and salvation revealed in the so-called servant songs of Isaiah – especially the fourth song (Isa. 52.13–53.12) – and the Christian identification of the servant as Jesus.

The biblical writer presents the saving logic of the servant's vicarious suffering in several steps. Anonymous persecutors inflict cruel torments on the servant. He breaks under the weight of his afflictions, while those who bear witness (including his tormentors) assume that God has rejected him. In line with their own theological presuppositions, they conclude that he was a sinner. Therefore, they bury him among sinners. But the inspired author intuits that the servant suffers for sins not his own. *He was pierced for our offenses, crushed for our sins; upon him was the chastisement that makes us whole, by his stripes we were healed* (53.5). Because he willingly suffers for the sake of others and as a result of their sins, the Servant achieves a victory that could not have been imagined or predicted, a victory only God could have produced. *Because of his affliction he shall see the light in fullness of days; through his suffering, my servant shall justify many, and their guilt he shall bear* (53.11). The victory of the servant is salvation – the forgiveness of sins and the justification of the guilty. The medium of salvation is the servant – the victim of the sin of the world. The possibility of redemptive solidarity emerges from the divine necessity of mercy. Ellacuría writes:

> Only in a difficult act of faith is the singer of the servant songs able to discover the very opposite of what appears to the eyes of history. Precisely because he sees one who is burdened by sins he did not commit, as well as the consequences of those sins, he dares by reason of the very injustice of the situation to attribute all that is happening to God. God can do no less than attribute to this act of absolute historical injustice a fully salvific value. God can make this attribution because the servant himself accepted his destiny of saving those who caused his sufferings by bearing those same sufferings.[13]

The theology of the servant reaches new heights when it is applied to the life and death of Jesus. At the same time, it provides an important way to address the first basic question of historical soteriology: 'How is the salvation of humankind achieved starting from Jesus?'[14] Like the servant, but in way that radicalizes the connection between salvation and historical suffering, Jesus first struggles against sin before dying because of it. This is crucial. It indicates that the salvific power of Jesus' death and resurrection is connected to his life. Jesus did not simply suffer and die. He was tortured and killed by the enemies of God's reign because he unmasked and subverted them. So, too, the resurrection not only reveals God's power over death but God's victory over injustice. *I, the Lord, have called you for the victory of justice. I have grasped you by the hand: I have formed you and set you as a covenant of the people, a light for the nations* (Isa. 42.6). The one whom God calls for the 'victory of justice', whom God raises up as a 'light for the nations', is none other than the one who was crucified.[15]

The light of salvation mediated by Jesus through his concrete history does not cease being historical after his resurrection. Rather, it must continually be renewed, embodied, and effected in a history marred by ongoing crucifixions. This generates a second key question for historical soteriology. 'Who continues in history this essential function, this saving mission that the Father entrusted to the Son?'[16] Ellacuría's response extends to the crucified people the line of reasoning linking Jesus and Isaiah's servant. The people appears not only as victim of the sin of the world, but as the world's judge and saviour. It appears in history as *judge* in so far as its 'judgment is salvation, in so far as it unveils the sin of the world by opposing it, in so far as it makes possible the redoing of what has been done badly, and in sofar as it proposes a new exigency as the unavoidable way to achieve salvation'.[17] This people appears in history as history's *saviour* in so far as it epitomizes the crucified body of Christ, in so far as it sheds light on the cruelty of the present world order, in so far as it illuminates the praxis by which the church faithfully fulfills its vocation, and insofar as it bears witness to the resurrection.

To sum up, by its correspondence to Jesus, the servant and martyr, the crucified people appears as light for the nations, a light with multiple facets. As a sign of contradiction, it calls the nations to conversion. As a revelatory place, it unveils God's triumph, the resurrection of the crucified one. As a servant, it embodies the 'hope against hope' that God vindicates the victim who bears the sin of the world. In all these ways, the crucified people points to Jesus, who in turn directs the eyes of faith to the God who saved him from death. Thus, through the very negativity of its suffering and death, the crucified people reveals the God who saves. Precisely here we encounter the central charism of the martyr.

Notes

1. See Mark 10.31; Luke 6.20; Matt. 25.40; Mark 8.35.
2. Ellacuría refers to two of his most important theological contributions as 'essays

in historical soteriology'; see Ignacio Ellacuría, 'El pueblo crucificado: ensayo de soteriología histórica', in I. Ellacuría et al., *Cruz y resurrección: anuncio de una Iglesia nueva*, Mexico City: CTR 1978, pp. 49–82, trs. P. Berryman & R. Barr as 'The Crucified People', in I. Ellacuría & J. Sobrino (eds), *Mysterium Liberationis*, Maryknoll: Orbis 1994, pp. 580–603, and 'Utopía y profetismo desde América Latina: un ensayo concreto de soteriología historíca', *Revista Latinoamericana de Teología* 17 (1989) pp. 141–84, trs. James Brockman as 'Utopia and Prophecy in Latin America', *Mysterium Liberationis*, pp. 289–328.
3. Ignacio Ellacuría, 'Discernir 'el signo' de los tiempos', *Diakonía* (no.17, 1981), pp. 57–59.
4. For a treatment of the crucial phrase 'historical reality', see Ignacio Ellacuría, *filosofía de la realidad histórica*, San Salvador: UCA Editores 1990; 'Hacia una fundamentacíon filosófica del método teológico latinoamericano', *Escritos teológicos*, San Salvador: UCA Editores 2000, pp. 187–218; Kevin F. Burke, *The Ground Beneath the Cross: The Theology of Ignacio Ellacuría*, Washington, DC: Georgetown University Press 2000, pp. 43–97; Georges De Schrijver, 'The Distinctive Contribution of Ignacio Ellacuría to a Praxis of Liberation: 'Shouldering the Burden of Reality'', *Louvain Studies* 25 (2000), pp. 312–35.
5. Jon Sobrino, *Christ the Liberator: A View from the Victims*, trs. Paul Burns, Maryknoll: Orbis 2001, p. 4.
6. Ignacio Ellacuría, 'The Crucified People', p. 590.
7. Ellacuría refers to the crucified people as *theological place* to highlight its contribution to the 'rethinking' of faith; see Ignacio Ellacuría, 'Los pobres, lugar teológico en América Latina', *Misión Abierta*, no. 4–5 (1981), pp. 225–40. Prior to the properly theological moment of reflection and corresponding to the action of faith itself, or what the mystics might call 'spiritual consolation', one can speak of a corresponding *theologal* place, spiritual place, or as I prefer in this context, *revelatory place*.
8. Ignatius Loyola, *The Spiritual Exercises of Saint Ignatius*, St Louis: Institute of Jesuit Sources 1992, #53.
9. Ellacuría, 'Las Iglesias latinoamericanas interpelan a la Iglesia de España', *Sal Terrae* 826 (1982), p. 230.
10. Ignacio Ellacuría, 'Lectura Latinoamericana de los *Ejercicios Espirituales* de San Ignacio', *Revista Latinoamericana de Teología*, 23 (1991), pp. 113, 115; see also J. Matthew Ashley, 'La contemplación en la acción de la justicia: La contribución de Ignacio Ellacuría a la espiritualidad cristiana', *Revista Latinoamericana de Teología* 51 (Sept./Dec. 2000), pp. 211–32.
11. This insight corresponds to what Edward Schillebeeckx calls an experience of negative contrast; see *Jesus: An Experiment in Christology*, New York: Seabury 1979, pp. 621–22; *God the Future of Man*, New York: Sheed & Ward 1968, pp. 153–54; see also Roger Haight, 'The Logic of the Christian Response to Social Suffering', in M. Ellis & O. Maduro (eds), *The Future of Liberation*

Theology: Essays in Honor of Gustavo Gutierrez, Maryknoll: Orbis 1989, pp. 139–53.
12. Ellacuría, 'The Crucified People', p. 591, trs. emended.
13. Ellacuría, 'The Crucified People', p. 598, trs. emended.
14. Ellacuría, 'The Crucified People', p. 580.
15. Jon Sobrino, *Jesus in Latin America*, Maryknoll: Orbis 1987, p. 148.
16. Ellacuría, 'The Crucified People', p. 580.
17. Ellacuría, 'The Crucified People', p. 603, trs. emended.

The Hope Born of the Martyrs' Love

JUAN HERNÁNDEZ PICO

I. The paradox of martyrdom

The death of martyrs does not engender hope from the start. It rather produces a deep frustration, an indescribable horror, a sharp anger, a fearful feeling of defencelessness, and serious discouragement: 'There were many who were astonished at him' (Isa. 52.14). This is the paradox of martyrdom. This is the case because today the death of martyrs represents primarily the triumph of powerful criminal violence, of state terrorism, which silences a prophet's voice for ever, brutally interrupts a reformer's project, mercilessly cuts short the life of a researcher, permanently extinguishes the thoughts of a genius, or humiliates and rapes the dignity of a community. The death of martyrs is the triumph of intransigence, lies, and self-aggrandisement. Behind – and logically and really before – the death of a martyr lies a murder that is both its material basis and the cruel and merciless face of unjustified institutional violence.

Oscar Romero, Archbishop of San Salvador, was a prophet. From his barricaded cathedral, the archbishop of the poor denounced, with the lucidity and bravery of a prophet, the structurally unjust, and therefore anti-Christian, situation of his country. Romero, a weak man transfigured by God's strength, filled the futureless people with hope, sowed dignity in despised hearts, welcomed the cries of his people with love, and above all helped to change the image of God, from a God always on the side of the rich and powerful to a God who prefers the poor and the weak, not because he excludes anyone but because he cannot tolerate the denial of his kingdom through the denial of bread to his starving brethren. Romero proved intolerably inconvenient and was murdered despite being a bishop (October 1980). With his death, the voice in his cathedral was extinguished and shed no further light on the situation in his country. The massacre that crowned his funeral finally secured the muzzle. An apocalyptic fury was unleashed on the country; its symbols were the people hanged in the district of Sumpul and the massacre of the population of the village of El Mozote.

Adolfo (known as 'Fito') Mijangos, an FUR member of Congress in Guatemala, was a reformer. From his wounded soldier's wheelchair he introduced a new language, one of vibrant rationality and indomitable passion for the truth. He could not bear the deceitful shows or the self-aggrandisement of the President General, nor the equating of the nation with the land of the oligarchs and their guardians, nor the trampling of human rights beneath the cloak of defending state security. His social democrat affiliation and lawyer's gift for placing the law at the service of justice showed him to be a new type of member of Congress, a true representative of the people. In the street, in his wheelchair, several bursts of machine-gun fire put an end to Fito's life, even though he was a wounded soldier. Eloquent defence of truth and justice was not heard again in the Congress of Guatemala for a long time.

Myrna Mack, co-founder of a centre for social research (AVANCSO) in Guatemala, was a lover of research as a sharp instrument for piercing through layers of a situation until its truth was discovered. She was a disciple of the Maryknoll Sisters, also passionate seekers after justice, and also of Joaquín Noval, a magnificent Guatemalan anthropologist who joined the Communist Party in 1954 after the United States helped to put a violent end to the first experiment at democracy in Guatemala. Also a disciple of the Jesuit Ricardo Falla, an excellent anthropologist and pastor of the 'Communities of Resistance Centres' during the armed conflict in Guatemala, Myrna was a free butterfly trying out her freedom of research in order to reveal the desperate situation of the people displaced by war and under attack from hunger as well as bombardments by the army. Despite her personal struggles with the faith, she was also the bishop of El Quiché's best adviser. The army regarded her research as a crime against state security and branded her an 'enemy within'. She was stabbed twelve times as she left her office one day in 1990, despite being a woman, in order to sow terror among social scientists and to restrict research.

Ignacio Ellacuría, Jesuit philosopher and theologian, rector of the Central American University of San Salvador, was a creative and transforming genius. He proposed to re-fashion the apostolic service of the Jesuits of the Central American province by shaping the best instrument of their spiritual tradition, the *Spiritual Exercises*, into an instrument that the province would use as a collective. He then proposed to do the same with the university as an institution. And finally he tried to do it with the country at war, putting forward ever new ideas as a basis for negotiation, for building a strong and autonomous civil society independent of the political parties, and for forging peace. His final proposal was even more daring: the creation of a civilization based on work rather than on capital, a civilization of poverty rather than of wealth, not a civilization of impoverishment but one in dialectic with the actual civilization of wealth, the wealth of those few rich people whose wealth cannot be universalized without destroying the planet and the human race with it. In short, nothing less than reversing the course of history regarded as irreversible. His visionary proposals were seen as communist, and he was regarded as the brains behind the guerrillas, even though he had subjected them to a critique that was both severe and public. Together with five other Jesuits and two women from their household, the army shot his head to pieces, even though it was an exceptional head. Today, in a world that is changing at increasing speed and in directions that could not be foreseen at the time of his assassination, we cannot count on a mind as brilliant as his to help us face history with transforming creativity.

In San Bartolomé Jocotenango, several hundred Quiché women were subjected to repeated rapes by army officers and soldiers and members of the Civil Self-Defence Patrols. More than a few of these women were forced into sexual slavery and held in prisons/brothels during the most brutal years of the war in Guatemala. Quite a number were wives of Catholic Action leaders who had questioned the unjust traditional activities of some chiefs of the indigenous population who acted as contractors for day labourers on the estates of landowners on the Coast. As for their husbands: 'Those who had a Bible were killed . . . the good men of Catholic Action'.[1] The choice these women, who witnessed the martyrdom of their husbands, fathers, and grandfathers, were forced to make was between rape and death. The rape of these women, even though some of them were wives or relatives of Patrolmen, was the symbol of the violation of the dignity of a whole people. Still today the patronal festival of St Bartholomew in August is desecrated and turned into a festival of exaltation of the army, while the priest says Mass behind locked doors.

Martyrdom is above all the triumphant affirmation of the most unjust powers of this world. This is why Jesus said to those who arrested him on the eve of his own martyrdom, 'This is your hour, and the power of darkness!' (Luke 22.53). Martyrdom is first the product of that deep enmity with humanity in which all death shares and which will not be destroyed until the end of history: 'The last enemy to be destroyed is death' (I Cor. 15.26). This is why Péguy's Joan of Arc, anticipating her own martyrdom, calls for a saint 'who will succeed', since 'everything comes, Lord, except your kingdom'.[2] Hope is not cheap, as Bonhoeffer said of grace.

II. The hope of martyrdom is against all hope

The hope born of the love martyrs bear for their fellows is none other than the hope of Abraham and of Jesus of Nazareth, since it is absolutely 'hoping against hope' (Rom. 4.18). It is not an easy or a cheap hope. It is a hope that has no signs or guarantees on which to depend. It does not count that Mgr Romero's prophetic quality and pastoral depth shone out with no shadows. Nor does it count to have unrestrained admiration for the reforming bravery of Fito Mijangos, or to be tenderly and unreservedly moved by the loving clarity of Myrna Mack. It matters not that we are attracted and wholly fascinated by Ignacio Ellacuría's bold vision, nor that we are violently indignant at the fate visited on the defenceless and enduring women of San Bartolomé Jocotenango. And above all it counts for nothing that the immense humble love that sustained all these people in their bids for justice, in their compassion for their brothers and sisters in humanity, and equally in their impotent resistance to injustice, should be obvious to all sorts of people. What matters is rather that these loves and the history they produced should open a path through the darkness until they become a blazing torch illuminating many lives and filling them with hope.

Both aspects are crucial. The love that inspired the lives of the martyrs is crucial. Martyrs can engender hope in people simply because they can dispose those who call themselves Christian and those who cannot confess God to take their commitment and communion with human beings, especially the most afflicted, despised and unjustly impoverished among them, to the extreme of giving their life for them, allowing it to be taken from them. The actual course of the martyrs' life inspired by love is also crucial. Because the powers of the world do not take anyone's life unless he or she has tried to construct a historical project that goes against the grain of the worst emotive aspects of culture, against the most deeply entrenched economic and political injustices, and for a new society moving, even if only in fits and starts, towards the kingdom of justice, of freedom, and of respectful encounter between cultures and religions.

The fact is that these loves and the history they aspire to construct have to make their way through dense darkness if the hope they promise is to come to birth. This darkness has a depressing overall feature: the failure of the historical projects to which the martyrs committed themselves and the concomitant frustrating abandonment in which those individuals on whom the martyrs bestowed their love have been left.

The vision of what it means to be a bishop so blindingly provided by

Oscar Romero now lies in tatters like his body shredded by the assassin's bullets. The Salvadoran people to whom he showed an inexpressible pastoral love are now governed with dispassionate prudence.

The figure of the incorruptible Congressman, spokesman for the Guatemalan people, embodied so completely in Fito Mijangos, has been disfigured by the bullets that destroyed his heart and his stomach. The Guatemalan people whom he represented with such dignity have been derived of his daily unconditional commitment to their service.

The proposal for truly rigorous and committed investigation into the situation, such as Myrna Mack tried to establish, has to go on being made today, at the same risk of life. Her daughter, her grandchildren, her parents and her siblings, together with so many displaced people for whom she represented the chance of an attentive and respectful hearing, full of communion with their sufferings and longings, have been left deprived of her love and friendship.

Ignacio Ellacuría's proposals for a civilization more of work than of capital, for a civilization of poverty rather than of wealth, and for a possibility of turning back the inhuman course of history, have found no effective following to make the seed corn of his bold genius bear fruit. Those of us who experienced his unconditional friendship and the always imaginative fire of his apostle's heart have been left deprived of the heat that, despite his sometimes arrogant shyness, so often penetrated our bodies.

The thinking of the women of San Bartolomé Jocotenango and their husbands and their fervent desire to 'come together' and work 'for things to change . . . for the bad times to change', to 'join together for life', to 'tell the word what is in our hearts . . . tell what happened in life . . . [tell that] we are all equal . . . we are all human. No matter where people come from, what language they speak, what words they say . . .'[3] were brutally flattened and humiliated by the rape of the women of the town. And the rapes destroyed the life of love: 'People no longer speak . . . There's hardly anything left to us, a bit of sadness . . . we don't sleep at night, we suffer for all the families, we suffer a lot . . . We are afraid, yes, afraid . . . we don't know what's going on . . . they are completely senseless . . . we are not going to understand . . . no, there's no life there . . . we feel there is no life since . . . the times have changed.'[4]

We have somehow to rescue hope from these shadows of failure and abandonment. All hope, including that which springs from the blood of the martyrs, is a responsible human task carried out breathing in the atmosphere of grace, of free gift. The new society and the new history of which the martyrs dared to dream, for which they longed and planned, are a new creation that we have to rescue and use our creativity to make productive, as we would with an inheritance. But the old creation has proved resistant, and it is in this, as in the time of Paul, that hope keeps inspiring our rescue work so that 'the creation itself will be set free from its bondage to decay and will obtain the freedom of the glory of the children of God' (Rom. 8.21). All this takes place accompanied by labour pains, and we are not exempt from groaning 'while we wait for adoption, the redemption of our bodies' (8.23). Ultimately, the hope that is born of the blood of the martyrs is not a 'hope that is seen', since we do not hope for what is the evidence of our eyes, but a hope in the midst of darkness, and so one that we need to 'wait for ... with patience' (8.24–25).

III. The hope born of the love of the martyrs: a work of constancy

The love of the martyrs leads to the birth of hope. How? Through our patient and responsible work, so through our constancy, which is a graced human activity very similar to fidelity. The initial part of this activity is redemption of the memory of the martyrs. Jesus of Nazareth seems to have been concerned that his memory should not be extinguished. He charges his disciples to eat his last supper, which anticipates his death, in the community of those who follow him: 'Do this in remembrance of me' (Luke 22.9; I Cor. 11. 24–25). From then on Christian liturgy will always be a proclamation of 'the Lord's death until he comes' (I Cor. 11.26); that is, it will be focussed on the memory of the assassination of Jesus, which was also his martyrdom, his testimony of a love greater than any other, laying down 'one's life for one's friends' (John 15.14). But at the same time no liturgical commemoration can be called Christian, says Paul, if it does not impel us to live daily that paradigm of the martyr that Jesus is: 'to present your bodies as a living sacrifice, holy and acceptable to God, which is your spiritual worship' (Rom. 12.1). From a very early age the relics of martyrs were embedded in the altar table, linking them to the Lord's supper. A constant memory of the martyrs that will lead to offering one's own existence, 'whether in tireless daily commitment or in sacrifice unto death violently suffered',[5] as Ellacuría himself wrote in the year of his martyrdom, is a service to hope.

The subsequent part of this activity consists in redeeming the truth suppressed by wickedness (cf. Rom. 1.18). All martyrdoms have been inseparably either murders or brutal attacks that, even when they involved torture that has not actually killed, have humiliated people and pushed them to the limit of endurance. Attempts have been made to cover up all these murders under the veil of accusations that supposedly justify them: 'He has blasphemed!' (Matt. 26.65); 'We found this man perverting our nation . . . He stirs up the people' (Luke 23.2, 5); 'If this man were not a criminal, we would not have handed him over to you' (John 18.30). With our modern martyrs, the same justifications are repeated: 'he was a Communist', 'a subversive', 'the brain behind the guerrillas'; 'she was an enemy of the state'; 'the bishops and priests lie . . . they say religion is not good'; 'all members of Catholic Action are guerrillas'.[6]

This is why the work done by Helen Mack, our martyr Myrna's sister, who has battled in the courts for twelve years to unmask the cover-up, to have her sister's physical and intellectual murderers judged and sentenced, and has eventually succeeded, is a paradigmatic example of that constancy with which hope can be rescued. Another example of rescuing hope was the work done by the Jesuit Central American provincial superior, José María Tojeira, with the support of the Lawyers' Committee of the USA and of civil lawyers who risked their lives, to arrive at the truth and see justice done to the murderers of Ignacio Ellacuría and his companions in martyrdom. This is a rescue task that is still looking for the intellectual authors of the crime carried out by subordinates.

A great work of rescuing hope was the *magnum opus* of Bishop Juan Gerardi, *¡Guatemala, nunca más!* ('Guatemala, Never Again!'), compiled with the precise aim of redeeming the historical memory of victims and martyrs, and he himself was assassinated, a martyr to truth, forty-eight hours after presenting the work in public. Another rescuing of hope has been the investigation carried out by Matilde González into the events at San Bartolomé Jocotenango, published by AVANCSO in two volumes under the title *Se cambió el Tiempo* ('The Times Have Changed', 2002). Human freedom is not possible without an encounter with the truth: 'If you continue in my word . . . you will know the truth, and the truth will make you free' (John 8.31–32). 'Continue' is a translation of the Greek verb *meinein*, which has the same root as *hypomoné*, meaning 'constancy'. The search for the truth about the crimes committed against the martyrs is another service to truth and an inescapable way of 'waiting with patience' for the redemption of truth. And it is in this way that 'the hope of the poor [will not] perish forever' (Ps. 9.18).

And it will not perish, because the love of those who underwent martyrdom and who today, after the first 'astonishment', like Jesus, still 'astonish' the world (Isa. 52.14), invites us to maintain our daily love with constancy, as it rejoices and sympathizes with 'the joys and the hopes, the griefs and the anxieties' of humankind, especially of 'those who are impoverished or in any way afflicted' (GS 1), in a work of solidarity guided by faith towards 'solutions which are fully human' (GS 11). The hope that sustained Jesus and his trusting faith in the Father, who appeared to have abandoned him, is the same hope that has sustained so many people to the point of martyrdom. Hope sustains faith and love. And then humble broken love, fragile and defeated, paradoxically victorious, brings hope laboriously to birth in us. This is the Christian circle. Neither deceit nor failure nor persecution nor the changing times can ever separate us from the love of those who have undergone martyrdom. Even though we have to inherit their love with creative constancy.

Translated by Paul Burns

Notes

1. M. González, *Se cambió el tiempo: Historias de vida* . . ., Guatemala 2002, pp. 34, 69.
2. Cited by C. Moeller, *Literatura del Siglo XX y Cristianismo, IV*, Madrid 1964, p. 595.
3. Cf. González, op. cit., p. 15.
4. Ibid., pp. 16–17, 108–9.
5. I. Ellacuría, 'Utopia and prophecy in Latin America' in I. Ellacuría and J. Sobrino (eds), *Mysterium Liberationis*, ET Maryknoll, NY 1993, p. 312.
6. González, op. cit., 68.

Martyrs: An Appeal to the Church

JON SOBRINO

Martyrs, taken all together as *Jesus martyrs*, who live and die like Jesus, and as *crucified peoples*, who live and die like the Servant of Jahweh,[1] offer light and salvation to the world and to the church, as has been said in previous articles. Here I want to dwell on the fact that they are also an appeal, which is good and necessary.

Compared with what happened at Vatican II, the universal church is going through a process of turning in on itself. It is true that there are numerous groups of Christians who share the pain of the world, who are prophetic and utopian, seeking to renew the spirit and the faith; it is also true that there are some Jesus martyrs today, above all in Africa. But as a whole the church is acting like an institution seeking 'pastoral success' (Pedro Trigo) in holding on to or recovering its social presence and weight. Compared to the church of Medellín, suffice to cite José Comblin's words:

> Today, the dominant impression is that the church, for the most part, the shepherds as well as the sheep, are going back to the past. It still speaks the same language, but the practice is different. It is drawing back into sacristies and parish houses. It no longer listens to the voice of the poor majorities, but to that of its traditional adherents, those who go to church services. The church is once more concerned with itself. It is seeking to recover positions of cultural, political, and even economic power. It is going back to cultivating religious feelings, emotions. There is no lack of takers, since the free-market model has led to a growth in anxiety, desperation, insecurity, and confusion among people.[2]

To reverse this turning inward it is not enough to recognize that the church is sinful, *casta meretrix*, and to ask forgiveness in the way that has been done in recent years by the pope himself, since the abstraction and lack of commitment with which it has been done has robbed such a confession of the church's own sins of its efficacy. The question then is what can appeal to the church.

God undoubtedly can, but on account of his transcendence, God can remain distant and his appeal go unheard; and, like all creatures, the church tries to make it so. Some years ago, at a time of vehement anti-Marxism, I wrote that 'the church is not afraid of Marxism, but of God'. Jesus Christ, the historical presence of the transcendent God, can also appeal, but Jesus too can be relegated to a distance from which he has no presence or capacity to appeal. And when it is suspected that he is seriously coming closer, then we can well have a repetition of the legend of the Grand Inquisitor: the cardinal-archbishop of Seville tells Christ, 'Lord, don't come back.'

But the Christian faith is resolutely incarnational. The church has to confess that Christ is present in the eucharist, in the celebration of the word, in the community and in its pastors. It can be appealed to through all these, although it can also ignore the appeal. But there is a final bastion – which is in effect the first – of the presence of God and his Christ: 'And with particular tenderness he chose to identify himself with those who are poorest and weakest [Matt. 25.40]' (Puebla 196). The poor are the greatest presence of Christ in history: 'vicars of Christ' they were called in the Middle Ages. They are therefore good news, and they evangelize the church; but they are also a summons, and they call the church to conversion (Puebla 1147). The *formal* reason for this has been stated: they are the presence of Christ. The *material* reason is that their clamour cannot be silenced (Medellín, *Justice* 1).

Let us go a step further. The poor and their clamours reach their highest expression in the *martyrs* – in the Jesus martyrs and above all in the crucified peoples – and this is what gives them the greatest capacity for appealing to the church. Quantitatively, they are so numerous that one would need to be blind and deaf not to notice them. Qualitatively, they give voice to such horrors that they can shake consciences – and also spur them to conversion. And, furthermore, they prevent us from using the deceitful excuse, to which the church is prone, that God alone can appeal to it, because God is in them.

This appeal by the *Jesus martyrs* makes itself heard more clearly at particular moments in history (the years following Medellín in 1968 were one of those times in Latin America, but also in Africa and Asia), although their appeal can always live on in their memory. The appeal by the *crucified peoples* is permanent, like the *mysterium iniquitatis* that runs through history.

I have provided a little theological tour to show what the deepest and most powerful root of the appeal to the church is, although this root – the poor, victims, martyrs – is clear to any heart of flesh. But I felt it had to be done in this way, bearing in mind that it is a matter of appealing to the church, which cannot defend itself against an appeal coming from them, since they are the greatest presence of God. And since it derives from them and not from anything else, this basic appeal will relate not to just anything but to the essence of the Christian faith: mercy, love, defence of the poor, and identification with the victims.

The conclusion is that the church can be appealed to, and, as Mgr Romero said, needs to be: 'We need someone to be a prophet to us too so as to call us to conversion, so that we are not allowed to install ourselves in a religion that then becomes untouchable' (Homily of 8 July 1979).

To end this introduction, let me say that what it shows is that the first and basic appeal to the church is on the very fact of whether it is prepared or not to allow itself to be appealed to. About what? About whether or not it resembles Jesus, about whether it follows Jesus in his incarnation, mission, cross, and resurrection. Let us look at this.

I. First appeal: the incarnation, 'overcoming irreality'

In this third millennium, the situation of the bulk of the inhabitants of our world is miserable. Their most difficult task is to live, and dying – in their bodies, their dignity, their culture, their spirit – is their closest fate. This means that the first thing the church has to do is to become incarnate in this reality in order to become 'real'.

This incarnation is not easy for the church, even though, according to its faith, it is an obvious and primary requirement. John's prologue expresses the *will* of God himself *to be real* in our world, a will that consists not simply in becoming actual flesh but in becoming weak flesh. And in the language of conciliar christology the reality the Son takes on is not simply *humanitas* but *sarx*, the weakness of the flesh. In Christianity, *transcendence* is, without a doubt, *trans-descendence* (Leonardo Boff). And this descending is to become not only 'the other' but 'the little and the weak'.

This is fundamental on the theoretical level, but it is not generally so in the life of the church. For the church (and not just for christology), the greatest problem here is *docetism* (Walter Kasper), that is creating its own sphere of reality (doctrinal, liturgical, canonical), which distances it and so defends it from the real world, and above all from its crosses. It is not easy to overcome this docetism, but at least we have to be conscious of our tendency to fall into it, of how unaware we are in the face of this reality. And then we have to be open to the challenge put by Antonio Montesino five centuries ago: 'How is it that you are sleeping in such depths of lethargic sleep?'

How can we open our eyes to reality and overcome this docetism, which is becoming virtually a historical embodiment? The miracle can be worked by the crucified peoples, who are crying out with inexpressible cries and calling us to come down. And the Jesus martyrs, who provide an example of doing so. So that there can be no way out, the latter show us the various ways in which this can be done in today's world: Martin Luther King from a social movement, Silvia Arriola from a grassroots community, Ignacio Ellacuría from a university.

For Archbishop Romero it was obvious that the church had, above all, to 'be real'. In defining words, some of them truly horrifying, he would say: 'I am happy, brothers, that the church is being persecuted, precisely on account of its preferential option for the poor and for trying to become incarnate in the concerns of the poor' (15 September 1979); 'It would be sad if, in a country where assassinations are on such a horrendous scale, we could not count priests too among the victims. They are the witnesses of a church incarnate in the problems of the people' (24 June 1979).

Anyone who might see sacrificialism or masochism in such words cannot not have understood either what life was like in El Salvador at that time or the depth of Romero's commitment to that reality. What he was saying was that a church that is not poor in a time of poverty, that is not persecuted at a time of persecution, that is not assassinated in a time of assassinations, that does not commit itself at a time for commitment and does not encourage commitment in times of indifference, that has no hope in a time of hope and does not raise hope in times of discouragement, is not a real church but a docetist church. It is good to formulate the ideal of the church as that of a *holy and authentic* church . . . But the be-all and end-all is first and foremost to be a *real* church.

Archbishop Romero's church could be accused of being a church with limitations, errors, and sins, but there could be no doubt that it was a 'Salvadoran', 'real' church. And not only from sharing in the suffering of the situation in El Salvador, but also in its spirit and creativity. 'You are such a lively church, so full of spirit!' It was a Salvadoran church, shot through with the generosity and commitment of its people.

Overcoming docetism has never been easy. The true *humanity* of Christ, even though it is evident from the New Testament, was defined at Chalcedon in 451, many years after his true *divinity*, which is less evident, had been defined at Nicaea in 325. There is something deep down in us that inclines us to docetism. The martyrs appeal to us and encourage us to move beyond it: the crucified peoples in themselves are a call for us to open our eyes to reality, the Jesus martyrs show us how to get involved in it.

II. Second appeal: mission, 'compassion for reality'

Medellín and Paul VI in *Evangelii nuntiandi* (30) made integral liberation an essential element in the church's mission. I should like to record here two aspects of this liberating mission, not just for the sake of setting them down mechanically but in order to appreciate the *pathos* of this mission, now dying the death of a thousand excuses.

The first is the *salvation of a whole people*. Archbishop Romero was defined by Ignacio Ellacuría as 'a man sent by God to save his whole people',[3] and Romero saw himself as the one who could speak for a whole people, 'the voice of the voiceless' (29 June 1979). Ellacuría insisted on the need to 'overturn history, subvert it, and re-launch it in a fresh direction',[4] and he formulated utopia as a new 'civilization of poverty'.[5]

The intent to work for 'a whole people' can be – or has been – more easily undertaken in some places (Latin America) than in others in which Christians are in the minority, and at some times – some decades back – than now. But what I want to stress here is the *ultimate purpose* of mission, which covers and embraces all aspects of the life and dignity of the oppressed majorities: the kingdom of God, the human family. The churches, big and small, have to take this into account and to act as an effective leaven. This was the purpose of many churches – Brazil is perhaps the best example – but the tendency now is to concentrate on and provide for individual salvation, or family salvation at best – good and necessary – rather than on that of a whole people, on interior rather than historical salvation.

The second is the *dialectical, prophetic pathos*. The proclamation of the kingdom was consubstantial with the denunciation of the anti-kingdom, which is what gave rise to conflict. Today mission is not placing the church, as a whole, in serious confrontation with the oppressive powers, although there are some skirmishes. Postmodernity, with its allergy to the grand narrative, may be exercising its influence here, as is the ideology of globalization, which ignores dialectic so as to canonize – almost always hypocritically – dialogue and tolerance, which almost of necessity degenerate into indifference to the poor. But a church that does not do its utmost for the defence of the majority, that does not struggle or engage in conflict on their behalf, becomes a closed sect or, indeed, a massive institution, but one detached from reality, a new attempt at socio-cultural Christendom.

Even with things as they are, the appealing subversive memory cannot disappear. Where are the prophecy, the homilies and pastoral letters of the 1970s and 1980s? What happened to that going out to the poor, sharing their impotence and their fate? In short, where is that first love of the church of Vatican II, concerning the dignity of every Christian within the church, and above all that of Medellín, concerning being a church of the poor?

Things clearly change, but neither the situation nor the gospel has changed to such an extent that the former *pathos* is now irrelevant. This *utopian, prophetic pathos of liberation* is nothing other than *the compassion induced by the crucified peoples*. It is not that the church no longer has anything of this, but it is kept more on the ethical than on the prophetic level: it seeks dialogue with other powers and avoids conflict with them; it speaks about evangelization a lot, but little about the *agonist* dimension of mission; it speaks about ecclesial communion, but not much about the kingdom of God as a table shared with the poor at its head. Comblin has said all this in vigorous and ironic words: 'The discourse of the preferential option for the poor is still repeated, but the practice is different. It is all just words . . . words, words, words. Before, the words said what was being done.'[6]

At present there are obviously *new* tasks for mission: gender, ethnicity, race, refugees, AIDS, ecology, intercultural and interfaith dialogue . . . And from the present we can look back on the limitations of the past: Comblin, for example, recognizes that liberation theology 'has not paid enough attention to the true drama of human beings, their destiny, their calling, and, as a result, to the basis of their freedom.'[7] But it is one thing to recognize the new elements of the present and the limitations of the past; it is quite another to ignore the *pathos* with which mission was formerly imbued: mercy and truth, against murder and lies (see John 8.44).

It is not easy to recover this *pathos*. There may even be – indeed there are – majorities of the poor who are not interested in it. We cannot ignore the fact that the church made an option for the poor, while these left, to a large extent, to join Pentecostal churches. But this should not be an excuse for failing to re-adopt the *pathos* of Medellín. 'The church of the poor is latent. A change of circumstance can bring it back up to the surface of history. Medellín will reappear tomorrow as a new ecclesial event.'[8] The question is whether this conviction exists in the church.

Sustaining the *pathos* of Vatican II and, from the Latin American viewpoint, that of Medellín above all, is a basic problem for the church of today, and the martyrs encourage it in this. The Jesus martyrs gave their lives not simply for good causes but for something deeper: the salvation of a whole *people*. The crucified *peoples* go on looking to the church for compassion, for it – together with many others – to work and struggle to take them down from the cross. They have had enough of alms and petty hand-outs, of

Martyrs: An Appeal to the Church

promises half-fulfilled or not at all, of unconcern and contempt, of deceitful promises of globalization that exclude them. And let us not forget that the church's very identity is at stake in the way it carries out its mission, since 'It is not the church that makes the mission, but mission that makes the church' (Moltmann).

III. Third appeal: the cross, 'taking on the burden of reality'

Reality is a heavy burden for the millions of victims and becomes a heavy burden for those who take their part. The crucified peoples demonstrate the first fact and the Jesus martyrs the second. I want to dwell on the latter now.

For the martyrs, taking on the reality was not mysticism or a simple desire to identify with the crucified Christ, but the outcome of following Christ; that is, of practising mercy to the end, which means not avoiding conflicts and risks. In a sense, Jesus' command to 'take up your cross and follow me' is tautological: being and doing like him – following him – leads to taking on what he took on – the cross.

In this sense, 'cross' means the suffering and death that follow from defending the oppressed and struggling against injustice, and it derives from the will to immerse oneself in the conflictivity inherent in unjust situations. By analogy, 'cross' can express other sufferings: anxiety, illnesses, failures, disappointments, fears, which can at times be even more painful than those that result from fighting for justice.

This should emerge clearly from the biblical-Jesus tradition. History is shot through with a theologal conflict between a God of life and the idols of death, which demand victims in order to survive. In John's theology the devil is not only a liar but also a murderer. Put like this, evil is not just evil but has the power to annihilate those who struggle against it. The great stumbling-block of history is that sin has power, and if this is the case, then the church has to take a stand against an evil that is conflictive.

This happens at times, and it certainly happened in Latin America in earlier periods. The church's mission was essentially conflictive, irrespective of personal opinions, through being incarnate in reality and defending the victims. Now, however, there is a lack of all this. There may be verbal confrontations between the hierarchy and the secular powers, but their words are generally measured, so that there may be *conflictive words and texts* but there are few *real conflicts*. There are exceptions, such as – to mention only martyr bishops – Archbishop Gerardi in Guatemala, Archbishop Isaías Duarte in Colombia, Archbishop Minzihirwa in the Democratic Republic of

Congo, but as a whole the church does not take up major crosses in order to say what it says or to do what it does, unlike the situation some years ago. Nor does it canonize these and many other martyrs of our times – which would lead it into conflict with their murderers, who are still alive. Furthermore, it seems to be seeking a return to a degree of harmony with the powers of this world. Several episcopal nominations in Latin America have been made with this purpose in mind.

We are told today that we must not be anachronistic, but I should add that neither must we be uncritical or self-deceiving. Both Christian faith and historical reality continue to be burdensome and conflictive. In any case, we have to retain something of Paul's *parresia* – courage, boldness, confidence – and not descend into cowardice. We must not put forward a fanaticized Christianity, but still less a watered-down version, one that ends by addressing victims and executioners on the same footing. We must not make Christianity a 'cheap grace', which, as Bonhoeffer said, is its greatest danger. We must not subliminally introject the cross – and, logically, the resurrection – as good things in liturgy and private devotion but with nothing serious to say about the reality the church has to take on. In this situation, the martyrs encourage us to take on the burden of reality, and in doing so they do us a great service.

In the first place, we have to recall that, although it is not a universal philosophical truth, it is a biblical and Christian truth that in order to redeem evil we have to combat it not only from without, through all legitimate and effective means, but also from within, taking it on ourselves. If we do not accept this, then the word of God on the suffering Servant and the crucified Christ are vain.

In the second place, taking on the cross bestows credibility on the church, which cannot be obtained by any other means, and proves that the church is acting in a Christian manner, since if what happened to *Jesus* does not happen to the church, to a large extent, there is no reason why it should be understood and accepted as *the church of Jesus*. This is what Romero thought: 'A church that is not persecuted but is enjoying the privileges and support of the world – this church should beware! It is not the true church of Jesus Christ!' (11 March 1979).

At times we are presented with outstanding examples of taking on reality, of staying within it, even in the knowledge that it is going to unleash its full force. This is the case of the seven Trappist monks of Thibirine, in Algeria, who despite all threats stayed in their monastery, which the prior, Christian de Chergé, had converted into a centre for Christian-Islamic dialogue. They were kidnapped and then, on 26 May 1996, murdered. Knowing their future, they stayed where they were. They were 'real' to the ultimate degree. Their example, and the words of Archbishop Romero cited above, represent the limit, obviously, but they show that the martyrs encourage us to take on the burden of reality – usually in a less extreme form.

The invitation to 'take up the cross' is as old as Christianity. It has never been easy, and it is not easy now. But it should at least remain a clear part of Christian theory, and we should not seek ways of avoiding it. What has never been easy is what the martyrs help us towards, and on which they, in any case, appeal to us. If the crucified peoples do not move the church to take on their suffering and share in their fate, nothing will do so. If the Jesus martyrs do not convince us that the greater love is possible and humanizing, and that its course lies through taking up the cross of reality, nothing will.

IV. Fourth appeal: resurrection, 'being carried along by reality'

I am formulating this section in conformity with the previous ones. The martyrs also appeal to/invite us to share in Jesus' resurrection.

Reality contains sin, which is why it is burdensome and we have to take it on ourselves. But reality also contains grace, which makes it a strength, one that can take us on itself. The martyrs – and all good people throughout history – impregnate reality with love and truth, which makes it lighter for us to take up and makes it powerful enough to take us up. This is why I am no longer talking simply about an appeal in the sense of challenge or questioning but about an invitation, an offer of grace. I would add, though, that it is not easy, even if it seems so, to *allow* ourselves to be taken on by reality, since *hybris*, human arrogance in not allowing ourselves to be graced, always makes its appearance. And this is why we have to keep talking of an appeal.

I relate this to the resurrection. This reality impregnated with love and truth makes it possible for us to live already as risen beings under the conditions of history. So that we do fall into 'angelicism', however, we do well to recall that the risen Christ's wounds had not disappeared: nor do they from those who live the resurrection in history. They are not transformed into celestial beings. But a graced reality makes it possible to live the following of Jesus with love, with the tinge of 'fullness' and 'victory' added by the resurrection. In historical terms, for the church and for Christian life, this means living with *freedom*, in the sense of triumph over self-centredness and selfishness, so that nothing stands in the way of doing good. Living with *joy*, in the sense of triumph over sorrow, so that suffering can produce not bitterness but purification. Living with *hope* against resignation, so that the mystery of iniquity, the not-yet, the certainly-not, and disappointment do not bury the promise . . . In this freedom, joy, and hope there is already a sort of reverberation of resurrection.

This is the invitation the martyrs offer the church. And on all accounts their final appeal is not to forget them. Not for their sake – they no longer live in a realm of self-interest – but for the needs of the church.

Conclusion

Let me say a final word about these needs. Vatican II warned us that 'believers themselves frequently bear some responsibility for this situation [of atheism] . . . [and] they must be said to conceal rather than reveal the authentic face of God' (*Gaudium et Spes*, 19). And scripture uses even stronger words of denunciation: 'On account of you the name of God is blasphemed among the nations.'

So then: the Jesus martyrs have not concealed the face of God but have revealed it through their lives and deaths. The name of God is not blasphemed in martyr churches but is blessed, or at least respected. Because of them we can say with gratitude, 'On account of you the name of God is blessed among the poor.' This applies to the world that looks to the church.

As for the crucified peoples, who also look to the church, only a church of Jesus martyrs that allows itself to be affected by them and regains its heritage will have any credibility for the crucified peoples and will keep alive their hope in its efforts to take them down from the cross.

Translated by Paul Burns

Notes

1. On this distinction see my other article in this issue: 'Our World: Cruelty and Compassion'.
2. 'Medellín ayer, hoy y mañana', *RLT* 46, 1999, pp. 79f.
3. 'Monseñor Romero: un enviado de Dios para salvar su pueblo', *RLT* 19, 1990, pp. 5–10.
4. 'El desafío de las mayorías pobres', *ECA* 493–4, 1989, p. 1078.
5. 'Utopía y profetismo desde América Latina', *RLT* 17, 1989, pp. 164–84.
6. 'Medellín', art. cit., p. 79.
7. *Called for Freedom*, Maryknoll, NY 1998, p. 197.
8. 'Medellín', art. cit., p. 81.

Open Letter to Our Martyrs

PEDRO CASALDÁLIGA

I write to all you men and women
who have given your lives for Life,
throughout the length and breadth of our America,
in streets and in mountains,
in factories and in fields,
in schools and in churches,
at dark of night or in the sunlight.
You above all have made our America
the continent of death with hope.

I write to you in the name of all our Nations and our Churches,
which owe you the courage to live, to defend their identities,
and the stubborn will to go on defending the Kingdom,
against the wind and the tide of the free-market anti-Kingdom
and despite the corruptions of our governments
or the involvement of our hierarchies
or our own surrenders.
We believe that while there is martyrdom there is credibility,
while there is martyrdom there is hope.

You, men and women, have washed the garments of your commitment
in the blood of the Lamb.
And your blood in his blood
still washes our dreams, our weaknesses
and our failures.
While there is martyrdom there will be conversion,
While there is martyrdom we shall see results.
The grain of corn can only multiply by dying.

I write to you in the face of prohibition
by the dictatorial powers – military, political or economic –
and in the face of the forgetful cowardice of our own Churches.

I write even though powers and Churches would impose
an amnesty that would be amnesia
and a reconciliation that would be surrender.
In vain.
You know how to forgive, but you want to live.
We shall not permit the supreme cry of your love to be stifled,
nor shall we allow your blood to be fruitless.

Nor shall we be superficially or irresponsibly content
with putting up posters of you,
with singing songs to you on pilgrimage,
with dramatizing you in plays.
We shall take on your lives and your deaths,
taking up your Causes.
Those specific Causes
for which you gave your life and death.
Those Causes, so human and so divine,
that in actual events and in effective charity
point to the greater Cause of the Kingdom,
for which the first-born from among the dead,
Jesus of Nazareth, crucified and raised for ever,
gave his life and his death, and for which he rose again.

We remember you all, men and women,
and we say none of your great names now
so that we can call to you all in one great shout
of love and commitment:
Our Martyrs! Women,
men, children, old people,
natives, peasants, workers, students,
mothers, lawyers, teachers,
pastoral workers, artists, writers,
pastors, priests, catechists, bishops . . .
Names that are known and already in our martyrology
or names unknown but written in God's roll-call.
We acknowledge ourselves your heirs, a witness Nation, a martyr Church,
deacons walking through the Continent's long Easter night,
so dark still, yet so unconquerably victorious.
We shall not yield; we shall not sell out; we shall not give up

this greater paradigm of our lives
that was the paradigm of Jesus himself
and is the dream of the Living God for all his children
throughout all time and in every nation
and in all worlds, towards the single and plural fellowship
of the Kingdom, the Kingdom – his Kingdom!

With St Romero of America and with all you men and women,
and all uniting in one voice and common purpose
with all the sisters and brothers whose solidarity goes with us,
we declare ourselves 'happy to run the same risks
[as you men and women were]
as Jesus, to identify ourselves
with the Causes of the dispossessed'.
And in this world prostituted by the global market and selfish wealth
we swear to you with humility and resolve:
'Far be it from us to glory
save in the cross of our Lord Jesus Christ'
and in your crosses that mirror his!
With him and with you all
we shall still hymn Liberation.
Through him and through you all
we shall jubilantly learn
that we too shall rise 'even at the cost of our lives'.

Translated by Paul Burns

Contributors

FELIX WILFRED was born in Tamilnadu, India, in 1948. He is professor in the School of Philosophy and Religious Thought, State University of Madras, India. He has taught, as visiting professor, in the universities of Nijmegen, Münster, Frankfurt am Main and Ateneo do Manila. He was also a member of the International Theological Commission of the Vatican. He has been president of the Indian Theological Association and Secretary of the Theological Commission of FABC. He is a member of the Board of Editors of *Concilium*. His researches and field-studies today cut across many disciplines in humanities and social sciences. Among his publications in the field of theology are: *From the Dusty Soil. Reinterpretation of Christianity* (1995); *Beyond Settled Foundations. The Journey of Indian Theology* (1993); *Sunset in the East? Asian Challenges and Christian Involvement* (1991); *Leave the Temple* (1992).

Address: University of Madras, Dept. of Christian Studies, Chepauk, Madras, India
E-mail: fwilfred@satyam.net.in

JON SOBRINO was born in the Basque Country in 1938 and educated in Spain; Germany, where he gained a doctorate in theology; and the USA, from where, unique among liberation theologians, he holds a master's degree in engineering mechanics. He joined the Society of Jesus in 1956 and since 1957 has belonged to the Central American province and lived mainly in El Salvador. His many works translated into English include *Christology at the Crossroads* (1976); *The True Church and the Poor* (1984); *Jesus in Latin America* (1986); *Spirituality of Liberation* (1988); *Companions of Jesus. The Murder and Martyrdom of the Salvadorean Jesuits* (1990). With the late Ignacio Ellacuría, he was joint editor of *Mysterium Liberationis: Fundamental Concepts of Liberation Theology* (1993). The first volume of his two-volume christology, *Jesus the Liberator*, appeared in 1993, and the second, *Following Jesus Christ*, in 2001.

ELSA TAMEZ was born in Mexico in 1950 and received her Doctor's Degree in Theology from the University of Lausanne, Switzerland. She received her Licenciate in Theology in 1979 from the Latin American Biblical Seminary, and received a Licenciate in Literature and Linguistics at the National University of Costa Rica in 1986. She is a faculty member of the Latin American Biblical University in Costa Rica and a member of the team of researchers of the Ecumenical Department of Investigation (DEI) in Costa Rica. Among her publications are: *Diccionario conciso Griego-Español* (1978); *Bible of the Oppressed* (1982), published in Spanish, English, Portuguese, French and Dutch; *The Scandalous Message of James* (1989), published in Spanish, Portuguese and English; *Amnesty of Grace* (1993), published in Spanish, English and German and *When the Horizons Close: Rereading Ecclesiastes* (2000), published in Spanish and English. She has also edited: *Against Machismo* (1987), published in Spanish and English; *Women's Rereading of the Bible* (1988), published in Spanish and English and *Through Her Eyes; Women Theologians from Latin America* (1989) published in Spanish and English.

Address: Universidad Bíblica Latinoamericana, Apartado 901–1000, San José, Costa Rica

TERESA OKURE, SHCJ, is Professor of New Testament at the Catholic Higher Institute of West Africa (CIWA). Formerly the Academic Dean of CIWA and Executive Secretary of EATWOT, she serves currently on the Executive Committee of the International Association for Mission Studies. She is author of *The Johannine Approach to Mission: A Contextual Study of John 4.1–42*, Tübingen 1988, and a commentary on John's Gospel for the International Catholic Bible Commentary, 1998.

Address: Catholic Institute of West Africa, PO Box 499, Port Harcourt, Nigeria
E-mail: Shcjokure@aol.com

SEÁN FREYNE is a former Director of *Concilium* and emeritus Professor of Theology at Trinity College, Dublin. He is currently Director of the Centre for Mediterranean and Near Eastern Studies at Trinity College. His most recent publications include *Galilee and Gospel. Collected Essays* (Brill

Paperbacks, Leiden and Boston 2002) and *Texts, Contexts and Cultures. Essays on Biblical Topics* (Veritas Publishers, Dublin 2002).

Address: 24, Charleville Road, Dublin 6, Ireland
E-mail: sfreyne@tcd.ie

JOSÉ IGNACIO GONZALEZ FAUS was born in Valencia in 1933. He is emeritus professor of theology at Barcelona University and academic dean of the 'Cristianismo y justicia' Study Centre in Barcelona. His more recent published works include: *La autoridad de la verdad. Momentos oscuros del magisterio eclesiástico* (1997); *Fe en Dios y construcción de la historia* (1998); *Proyecto de hermano. Visión creyente del hombre* (3rd edn 2000); *La Humanidad Nueva. Ensayo de cristologia* (9th edn 2000); *Acceso a Jesús* (9th edn 2000); *Migajas cristianas* (2000).

CARLOS MESTERS was born in 1931. In 1949 he went from the Netherlands to Brazil as a seminarian. He became a Carmelite in 1951. From 1954 to 1963 he studied in Rome and at the École Biblique in Jerusalem. Since 1963 he has been lecturing on the Bible in seminaries and Christian base communities; from the beginning he has been associated with the Ecumenical Biblical Centre (CEBI).

E-mail: cmesters@ocarm.org

GEORG EVERS was born in Emmerich in 1936. He studied philosophy in Munich (1956–61); Japanese language, history and culture in Kamakura (1962–64); theology at Sophia University in Tokyo (1965–69), obtaining a licentiate and MA in theology. From 1969 to 1972 he pursued his doctoral studies in theology in Münster under Karl Rahner on the theme 'Theology of Mission and Religions', and from 1973 to 1979 was a collaborator in ecumenical and adult education in Bendorf, near Koblenz. From 1979 to 2001 he was head of the Asia Desk of the Institute of Missiology in Aachen. During these years he travelled widely in Asia, actively participating in many of the theological conferences organized by the Federation of Asian Bishops' Conferences (FABC). He has published widely in the field of contextual theologies, inter-religious dialogue and theology of religions.

Address: Roetgenerstrasse 42a, 4730 Raeren, Belgium
E-mail: evers@skynet.be

Contributors

PETER KANYANDAGO (born in 1951) is currently Deputy Vice-Chancellor in charge of academic affairs at Uganda Martyrs University, where he is also Professor in the Institute of Ethics and Development Studies and Director of the African Research and Documentation Centre. He is a diocesan priest in the Mbarara Archdiocese, Uganda. He holds a doctorate from the Catholic University of Louvain-la-Neuve, Belgium. His main area of research is the interface between theology and anthropology, in which he has published widely.

Address: Uganda Martyrs University, PO Box 5498 Kampala, Uganda
E-mail: pkanyandago@umu.ac.ug

ALBERTO MELLONI teaches contemporary history at the University of Modena and Reggio Emilia; he is member of the XXIII Foundation for Religious Studies, Bologna, on the board of *Cristianesimo nella storia* and a member of the board of directors of *Concilium*. He has written extensively on the history and the institutions from the Middle Ages (*Innocenzo IV*, preface by B. Tierney, Genoa 1990) to the twentieth century: he worked on John XXIII (*Tra Istanbul, Atene e la guerra. A. G. Roncalli vicario e delegato apostolico 1935–1944*, Genoa 1993; *Il Giornale dell'Anima di Giovanni XXIII*, Milan 2000), on Vatican II (as editor of the five volumes of *Storia del concilio Vaticano II diretta da G. Alberigo*, Bologna 1995–2001), on Vatican II diplomacy (*L'altra Roma. Politica e S. Sede durante il concilio Vaticano II, 1959–1965*, Bologna 2000), and on the conclave (*Il conclave. Storia di una istituzione*, Bologna 2001). His articles in different journals are devoted to the interplay between politics and religion.

Address: Via Crispi 6, 42100 Reggio Emilia, Italy
E-mail: alberto.melloni@tin.it

KEVIN F. BURKE, SJ, was born and raised in Wyoming (USA) and entered the Society of Jesus in 1976 in Denver, Colorado. Following his ordination as a priest in 1986, he served as a faculty member and campus minister at Regis University in Denver where he co-founded the Mexico Project and Romero House. In 1997 he joined Weston Jesuit School of Theology in Cambridge, Massachusetts, where he is presently Associate Professor of Systematic and Historical Theology and director of the Licentiate in Sacred Theology degree programme. His first book, *The Ground Beneath the Cross: The*

Theology of Ignacio Ellacuría, elaborated the philosophical foundations and theological method underlying Ellacuría's historical soteriology and theology of the crucified people. He has recently published essays on Archbishop Oscar Romero and the martyrs of El Salvador, and is presently co-editing a collection of essays on Ellacuría's thought and editing a selection of the spiritual writings of Fr Pedro Arrupe, SJ.

Address: Xavier House, 80 Lexington Ave, Cambridge, MA 02138-3337
E-mail: kburke@wjst.edu

JUAN HERNÁNDEZ PICO, SJ, was born in 1936. He has been a Jesuit since 1953 and a priest since 1966. He studied theology at Sankt Georgen, Frankfurt, and sociology at the University of Chicago. He was Director of the Jesuit Centre of Research and Social Action in Central America (1980–90). He is Professor of Sociology and Theology at the Universities of Managua and San Salvador. His books include *Un Cristianismo Vivo*, *Teología de la Solidaridad* and *La Oración en los procesos de liberación*.

Address: Casa Parroquial, Santa María Chiquimula, 08006 Totonicapán, Guatemala, CA
E-mail: jhpico@infovia.com.gt

PEDRO CASALDÁLIGA was born in Spain of Catalan stock in 1928 and is a Claretian missionary. He has lived in Brazil since 1968 and in 1971 was ordained bishop in the Prelacy of São Félix do Araguaia, in the province of Mato Grosso. A poet and writer, he is also vice-president of the Pastoral Land Commission. His works include *Uma Igreja da Amazónia em conflicto com o Latifúndio e a Marginalizacão social* (1971); *Creo na Justiça e na Esperança* (translated into English); and *Tierra nuestra, Libertad*.

Address: Prelazia de São Félix do Araguaia, CX Postal 05, CEP. 78.670.000 S. Félix o Araguaia MT, Brazil

CONCILIUM

FOUNDERS

A. van den Boogaard
P. Brand
Y. Congar OP †
H. Küng
J.-B. Metz
K. Rahner SJ †
E. Schillebeeckx OP

FOUNDATION

Jan Peters SJ, President
Hermann Häring
Regina Ammicht Quinn
Christoph Theobald SJ
Ben van Baal, Treasurer

DIRECTORS

Regina Ammicht Quinn
Maria Pilar Aquino Vargas
Erik Borgman
Christophe Boureux OP
Hermann Häring
Hille Haker
Maureen Junker-Kenny
Alberto Melloni
Teresa Okure SHCJ
Jon Sobrino SJ
Janet Martin Soskice
Luiz Carlos Susin OFMCap.
Elsa Tamez
Christoph Theobald SJ
Miklós Tomka
Elaine Wainwright
Felix Wilfred
Ellen van Wolde

General Secretariat: Erasmusplein 1, 6525 HT Nijmegen, The Netherlands
http://www.concilium.org
Manager: Baroness Christine van Wijnbergen

Concilium Subscription Information

Forthcoming issues in 2003

February 2003/1: *Rethinking Martyrdom*
Edited by Teresa Okure, Jon Sobrino and Felix Wilfred

April 2003/2: *The Discourse of Human Dignity*
Edited by Regina Ammicht-Quinn, Maureen Junker Kenny and Elsa Tamez

June 2003/3: *'Movimenti' in the Church*
Edited by Alberto Melloni and Miklos Tomka

October 2003/4: *Learning from other Faiths*
Edited by H Haring, J Soskice and Felix Wilfred

December 2003/5: *Reconciliation in a World of Conflicts*
Edited by Luis Carlos Susin, Maria Pilar Aquino and Jon Sobrino

New subscribers: to receive *Concilium 2003* (five issues) anywhere in the world, please copy this form, complete it in block capitals and send it with your payment to the address below.

Please enter my subscription for *Concilium 2003*

Individuals
____ £29.00 UK/Rest of World
____ $57.00 North America

Institutions
____ £48.50 UK/Rest of World
____ $93.50 North America

Please add £15.00/$22.50 for airmail delivery

Payment Details:
Payment must accompany all orders and can be made by cheque or credit card
I enclose a cheque for £/$ _____ Payable to SCM-Canterbury Press Ltd
Please charge my Visa/MasterCard (Delete as appropriate) for £/$ _____
Credit card number _____
Expiry Date _____
Signature of cardholder _____
Name on card _____
Telephone _____ E-mail _____

Send your order to *Concilium*, SCM-Canterbury Press Ltd
9-17 St Albans Place, London N1 0NX, UK
Tel +44(0) 20 7359 8033 Fax +44(0) 20 7359 0049
E-Mail: office@scm-canterburypress.co.uk

Customer service information:
All orders must be prepaid. Subscriptions are entered on an annual basis (i.e. January to December) No refunds on subscriptions will be made after the first issue of the Journal has been despatched. If you have any queries or require information about other payment methods, please contact our Customer services department.

www.ingramcontent.com/pod-product-compliance
Lightning Source LLC
Chambersburg PA
CBHW070643300426
44111CB00013B/2232